Where Do You Park an Ark?

BIBLEQUEST
DEVOTIONS FOR TEENS

Where Do You Park an Ark?

RICK BLANCHETTE

Tyndale House Publishers, Inc. Wheaton, Illinois

Library of Congress Cataloging-in-Publication Data

Blanchette, Rick,   date
   Where do you park an ark? / Rick Blanchette.
      p.   cm. — (Bible Quest)
   ISBN 0-8423-1346-X
   1. Bible stories, English. [1. Bible Stories.] I. Title.
II. Series.
BS551.2.B54   1994   94-9714
220.9′505—dc 20

Printed in the United States of America

99   98   97   96   95   94
 9   8   7   6   5   4   3   2   1

For my parents,
Curt and Roxanne,
who encouraged me
when I was a teen;
and for my wife,
Ronda,
who tolerates me
now that I'm a grown-up.

Contents

Introduction

Welcome to Bible Quest!

As you read through the stories, you will notice that this is a different sort of devotional book. Most devotions focus only on making us better people (which isn't a bad thing). Then there are Bible study books that teach us about the Bible (which isn't bad either). But if we want to do both—become better people *and* learn about the Bible—we have to read two books. This, of course, isn't necessarily a bad thing, but it does take a lot of time.

Bible Quest combines Bible study and devotional material in one convenient place. As we learn about people, places, and events in the Bible, we also read notes that help us apply what we're reading. The result? We learn about the Bible *and* learn how to be better people while reading only one book! Nifty trick, huh?

There are fifty-two readings, one for each week of the year. However, if you want to read more than one a week, that's fine. In fact, that's great! If you want to use these devotions in a weekly youth group, Bible study, or church school, that's fine. In fact, that's great! If you want to read one devotion a year until you retire, that's not fine. In fact, that's pretty wimpy!

As you read, have fun with the characters and places they go. Maybe even picture yourself with them as their stories unfold, standing beside them as you both make great discoveries about God, Jesus, and the Bible.

Let the quest begin!

1 · **Where Do You Park an Ark?**

Along, long time ago, long before any youth leader made you sing "Arky, Arky," lived a man named Noah. And we know about Noah because he did something remarkable: He was the only person of his day that God was happy with. In fact, he was the only person at the time who would be able to survive a great flood God was going to send to cleanse the world of its sin and crime.

So God told Noah, "I have decided to destroy all mankind; for the earth is filled with crime because of man. Yes, I will destroy mankind from the earth. Make a boat . . . 450 feet long, 75 feet wide, and 45 feet high. . . . Look! I am going to cover the earth with a flood. . . . All will die. But I promise to keep you safe in the ship, with your wife and your sons and their wives. Bring a pair of every animal—a male and a female—into the boat with you, to keep them alive through the flood."

And Noah set to work building the ark.

This must have been a strange sight, an old man building a huge ship on his property. But if this sight was strange to the evil people of the day, the reason Noah was building the boat must have seemed even stranger. A typical conversation between Noah and his neighbors might have gone like this:

Neighbor: So, Noah, that's some boat you have there.

Noah: You noticed it, did you?

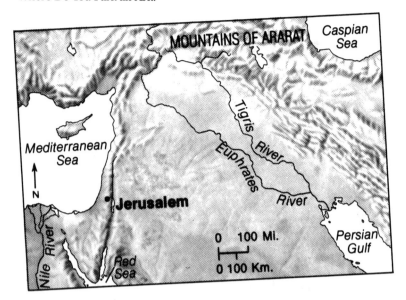

Neighbor: Yes, I did. Why are you building a 450-foot boat on dry land?

Noah: Because God told me he's sending a flood to destroy the world, and I need to save the animals and my family.

Neighbor: Oh. . . . When you're done, would you build me a barbeque pit?

....

Noah must have explained why he was building the boat, but we don't read of anyone repenting or asking God, or Noah, to save them. The people of that day were too evil, or God deemed it too late for them. Today is a different story. God doesn't want anyone to be separated from his Son and his love. If God gives you something to do and it seems out of the ordinary, maybe God is using that to attract people to you and to give you a chance to share your experiences with them. The earth will be destroyed again someday (see 2 Pet. 3), but this time God would like for everyone to be saved.

....

When the Flood did come, Noah had the animals on board (*how* he did it is something we'll have to ask in heaven!) and was ready. The rains came down day after day, and the water level rose, and Noah's neighbors surely wished they had taken Noah seriously.

After 40 days of rain, the whole earth was covered with water, and the ark floated for 150 days. We don't know how far Noah's boat traveled during that time. It may have stayed basically in the same spot, or Noah may have gone in any number of directions for any number of miles. The Bible only tells us where he wound up; it doesn't tell us where the starting point was.

It was after the 150 days that the ark did touch land, but that land was pretty high! Noah's ark had settled in the mountains of Ararat, which are in Turkey, near the border of the Soviet republics. Once the water had receded and the earth was livable again, the animals and Noah's family left the ark and moved south to the area where Iran and Iraq are today, which was possibly where he had lived before the Flood.

....

Noah had quite an adventure, and it wasn't a piece of cake! He faced hard labor, ridicule, and a smelly boat, but he had accomplished God's plan. Think about what could have happened had Noah not followed God. Would we even be here now? Think about the plans God has for us. What might (or might not!) happen if we refuse to obey?

....

2 · Abram's Journey to Canaan
GENESIS 11:27–12:9

Abram and his family lived in Ur of the Chaldeans, which is the southern portion of the modern-day country of Iraq. God spoke to Abram and told him to go wherever he would lead. So Abram, his father Terah, his nephew Lot, and his wife Sarai packed up their belongings and moved north, following the Euphrates River.

They traveled about six hundred miles to the city of Haran before they stopped and settled. They probably settled for a while because Abram's father was about two hundred years old and may have been too weak to go any farther. After Terah died, Abram got the message from God to move on. So he packed everything up again and moved south. God told him to stop when he got to the land of Canaan, where the nation of Israel would be someday.

....

Abram must have really loved God to be able to leave his home and go to a place that God was keeping a secret. Could you leave all your friends and move to some far away country?

....

When you look at the map of their trip, you can see that they didn't take a very direct path to Canaan. They went way up north and then came back south to reach Canaan. Abram could have gone straight west and saved four hundred miles of traveling. Why didn't he? Well, the land between Ur and Canaan is a large desert, and the trip across it would have been very dangerous. Abram and his family could have run

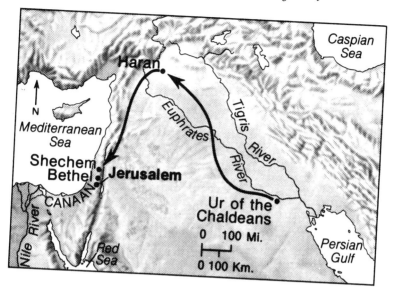

out of food and water on the way. Many
people who tried this route never made it. So they took a
much safer way to their new home. By traveling along the
Euphrates River, they knew they would have plenty of food,
water, and shelter.

After a very long trip, Abram came to the city of Shechem,
where God made a promise to him. God said, "I am going to
give this land to your descendants." At the end of Abram's
long journey God gave him a special gift—a huge area of
land for Abram and his descendants to live in.

....

While the trip itself was important, what really stands out is
that Abram obeyed God, even though he didn't know where
God would lead. Today we face the same challenge—to follow
God wherever he may lead us. And though he probably won't
lead us across a desert to found our own nation, we are called
to follow him every day. God might ask us to tell our friends in
school about him or to take an unpopular stand on some issue.
Our journey with God might require us to take more responsibility in church or youth group. Whatever it is that God asks of
us, we should be like Abram and pick ourselves up and follow
God, trusting him to help us as we travel with him.

....

5

3 · A Mount of Sacrifice

GENESIS 22:1-14

Have you ever gotten something that you really, really wanted, like a puppy, or a dirt bike, or a computer? If so, then you know how much that thing means to you, and how you'd rather die than give it up.

Well, take that feeling you are remembering and multiply it by 1200 and you will see how much Abraham loved what he had really wanted all his life—his own son. Isaac was born when Abraham was one hundred years old. He was no ordinary kid. He was the child through whom God promised to provide millions of descendants to Abraham. So not only was Isaac Abraham's son, he was a miracle and a gift from God.

Now imagine that thing that you really wanted, and imagine wanting it 1200 times more than you do, and then imagine someone asking you to get rid of it. *No way!* you're thinking. Now imagine that God asked you to give up that item. Would you be able to?

That's exactly what happened to Abraham. God spoke to him one day when Isaac was still a young boy and said, "Take with you your only son—yes, Isaac whom you love so much—and go to the land of Moriah and sacrifice him there as a burnt offering upon one of the mountains which I'll point out to you!"

And off Abraham went with Isaac the next day. No objections. No excuses. No lies. He just obeyed God and prepared to sacrifice the child he had waited one hundred years for.

The trip from Beer-sheba, where Abraham lived, to Mount Moriah was about fifty miles and took three days. That was plenty of time for Abraham to really think about what God had asked of him and to try to come up with a way out. But he did no such thing. Instead, when they arrived at Moriah, Abraham had the servants stay behind while he and Isaac went up the mountain.

"Father, we have the wood and the flint to make the fire, but where is the lamb for the sacrifice?" Isaac naively asked.

Sweat must have been running down Abraham's face as he struggled for an answer. He only said, "God will see to it, my son," and continued on up the mount.

Now the moment of decision was here. They were at the altar. They prepared the wood. Could Abraham go through with the plan?

The answer is yes. Abraham obediently tied up Isaac on the altar and held a knife over his son, ready to kill the boy.

But the Lord called to Abraham, "Lay down the knife; don't hurt the lad in any way, for I know that God is first in your life—you have not withheld even your beloved son from me."

....

Can you begin to think how hard this was for Abraham—to be on the brink of sacrificing something so precious? God had no intention of actually letting Abraham kill his son, but he wanted to make sure Abraham's faith was strong enough to trust him even when it was painful. Following God isn't always pleasant or easy. He may ask us to give up something that is important to us. Do we have the faith of Abraham to say, "OK, God. It's all yours"?

....

After God had spoken, Abraham saw a ram caught in a bush, and he sacrificed it instead, to the delight of a much-worried Isaac. This mountain, Mount Moriah, is located near the old city of Jerusalem and now is enclosed in modern Jerusalem. This mount would be central to the Jews as they became a nation. It was where King David sacrificed to God to stop a plague (see 2 Sam. 24 for this story). It was also on that spot that, as tradition tells us, the Holy of Holies in the Temple was built and where the curtain was ripped in two when God did what Abraham was spared—sacrificed his own Son.

4 · Jacob's Ladder
GENESIS 27:41–29:1

Have you ever done something to your brothers or sisters that made them so angry they yelled, *"I'm going to kill you!"?* You knew they wouldn't actually kill you, but you still thought it was wise to run as far as possible, just in case.

Jacob was in a similar situation. He had really ticked off his brother Esau by stealing his birthright and the blessing from their father, Isaac. Esau was the older brother, and the family blessing belonged to him. But Jacob, with the help of his mom, Rebekah, schemed to get the blessing (and the larger portion of the inheritance) for himself. And when Esau discovered what had happened, he saw red. He said, "My father will soon be gone, and then I will kill Jacob."

Esau wasn't just being dramatic; he *really* wanted Jacob dead. So Jacob did what any one of us would have done when an older sibling is after us: He ran. Rebekah spoke to Isaac and convinced him that Jacob should go to their relatives' region to find a wife, since Rebekah was "sick and tired of these local girls." Isaac agreed and sent Jacob off with a blessing.

....

So far, Jacob hasn't shown any of the traits that made his grandfather Abraham so great. He lied in order to steal his brother's blessing and inheritance, and then he ran away in fear. But God was going to use this for his purposes. He had promised Rebekah that Jacob would rule Esau (see Gen. 25:23) and would have arranged it in his own timing had not Rebekah

and Jacob plotted on their own. Their plan caused a bitter
rivalry that left the son who was to rule fleeing for his life. They
jumped the gun, but God still was able to work in the situation,
as we will see. We shouldn't get impatient when it comes to
God's promises. God will give us the opportunities to achieve
his plan for us—honestly.

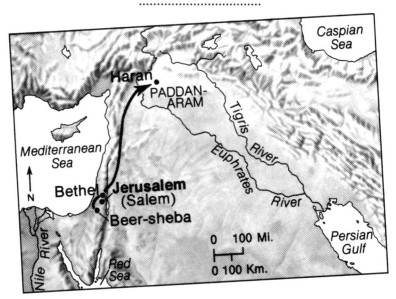

After his first day of run-
ning, Jacob camped near a town called Luz, which was just
north of Jerusalem and near the same place where Abraham
had set up an altar to God. Jacob went to sleep with his head
resting comfortably on a nice, soft rock when he had a dream
of a staircase leading to heaven.

At the top of the stairs was God, who said, "I am Jehovah, the God of Abraham, and of your father, Isaac. The
ground you are lying on is yours! I will give it to you and
to your descendants. For you will have descendants as
many as dust! . . . What's more, I am with you, and will
protect you wherever you go, and will bring you back
safely to this land; I will be with you constantly until I have
finished giving you all I am promising."

Terrified, Jacob woke up. "God lives here! I've stumbled into his home! This is the awesome entrance to heaven!"

The next morning Jacob took that comfortable rock and stood it on end and dedicated it as a memorial to God. He vowed, "If God will help and protect me on this journey and give me food and clothes, and will bring me back safely to my father, then I will choose Jehovah as my God! And this memorial pillar shall become a place for worship."

Before he left, he renamed that place Bethel, which means "House of God."

....

Of course God would keep him safe—wasn't he listening to his dream! Jacob's vow wasn't the conditional sort of vow many of us make today: "If I win the lottery, then I'll worship you, God." It was an affirmation that he would worship God in the future. Jacob didn't have to worry about what would happen to him because God said Jacob would have many children and that he himself would protect Jacob. When we have it straight from God's mouth, there's no need to worry. We have many promises from God that he will take care of us. Read Matthew 10:19-20, 29-31; 1 Corinthians 10:13; and Philippians 4:6-7 when you need to be reassured of those promises.

....

5 · **Family Reunion**

GENESIS 46:1-34

I f there were another name for the book of Genesis, it might be called the Book of Journeys. These patriarchs (Abraham, Isaac, and Jacob) really racked up the "frequent camel" miles, if you know what I mean. We've only seen a few of the more significant trips in Genesis, but the stories of the ones we missed are pretty thrilling, too. The last trip the people of Genesis made, to Egypt, was the last they'd make for four hundred years. And this trip to Egypt was planned years before by the divine Travel Agent himself.

It all started back in Genesis 37, when Joseph was having these dreams of his family bowing down to him. If he were the oldest son, this wouldn't have been a big deal, but he was the second youngest of twelve brothers. Obviously, the other brothers weren't going to stand to have Little Joey making such bold claims, so they decided to kill him. But brother Reuben convinced them to put him in a pit to die (intending to rescue Joseph). Then some traders came and bought Joseph from his brothers, and they in turn sold him to a master in Egypt. Well, to make a long, fascinating story short, Joseph became a ruler in Egypt and made plans to store food for the coming famine. (If you want to read all the juicy details, see Gen. 37:2-36; 39:1–41:57.)

This famine also struck in Canaan, where Jacob and the rest of his family had settled.

Jacob asked his sons, "Why are you standing around looking at one another? I have heard that there is grain available in Egypt. Go down and buy some for us before we all starve to death" (Gen. 42:1-2).

So Joseph's ten older brothers went to Egypt to buy grain.

Now we must remember that this wasn't like our mom giving us five dollars to pick up some milk and bread at the grocery store down at the corner—Egypt, and the city of Memphis where the administration was done, was over three hundred miles away. They made this trip not just once but a second time to buy more grain (and to get back Simeon, who was held hostage—you're gonna have to read Gen. 43–45 to find out why!).

Once all the brothers were in Egypt and in front of Joseph (whom they hadn't recognized), Joseph yelled to them, "I am Joseph! Is my father still alive? . . . I am Joseph, your brother whom you sold into Egypt! But don't be angry with yourselves that you did this to me, for God did it! He sent me here ahead of you to preserve your lives. . . . Hurry, return to my father and tell him, 'Your son Joseph says, "God has made me chief of all the land of Egypt. Come down to me right away!

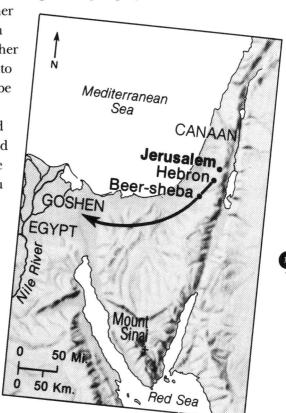

You shall live in the land of Goshen so that you can be near me with all your children, your grandchildren, your flocks and herds, and all that you have. I will take care of you there.'"

When Joseph's brothers returned to Canaan and told their father the news and showed him all the stuff Joseph sent, Jacob was thrilled! "Joseph my son is alive! I will go and see him before I die."

So Jacob gathered the family together and headed on down to Egypt. On the way, Jacob offered a sacrifice to God in Beer-sheba, and God spoke to him there in a dream.

"I am God," the voice replied, "the God of your father. Don't be afraid to go down to Egypt, for I will see to it that you become a great nation there. And I will go down with you into Egypt and I will bring your descendants back again; but you shall die in Egypt with Joseph at your side."

That was good enough for Jacob, who continued on to Egypt, had a teary reunion with Joseph in the land of Goshen, and settled there for the rest of his life.

·····························

If anyone had asked Joseph in the early years of his slavery why his brothers had sold him, he might have said it was because they were jealous bullies. It took many years for God's plan to become apparent. Sure, when he was younger he had dreams of leading his family, but those years of sitting in prison (which you have to read about; I didn't tell that part of the story) must have seemed to make those dreams impossible. Still, they came true. People for years have said, "God works in mysterious ways," and I'm sure Joseph would have said a hearty amen to that. So when our life seems up in the air or just plain rotten, we can focus on Joseph and how God worked through his problems to save his family. Like Joseph, we can keep looking to God because he knows why all this stuff is happening. Sooner or later it will make sense.

6 · From Prince to Shepherd

EXODUS 2:1-25

I f there had been a post office in the Egyptian city of Rameses, Moses' picture would have been on the bulletin board with the notice reading, "WANTED: MOSES, for the murder of an Egyptian while the Egyptian was innocently abusing a slave. Considered dangerous. Ten-horse reward for information leading to the arrest and execution of Moses."

This was quite a fall for a man who may have possibly become one of the pharaohs of Egypt. For though Moses was a Hebrew (whether or not he was aware of this is unknown to us), he was actually raised by one of Pharaoh's daughters after she found him in a basket on the Nile. Since Hebrew children were supposed to be killed, per Pharaoh's order, we can guess that Pharaoh's daughter somehow kept Moses' identity hidden from her father and raised him in the royal court.

The turning point in Moses' life came when he was out watching the Israelite slaves one day. He saw a very troubling sight—an Egyptian was beating a slave. Moses couldn't just sit idly by, either because his sense of decency wouldn't allow it or because he indeed knew he was related to the Hebrews. So, looking around to make sure the coast was clear, Moses attacked and killed the Egyptian and then hid the body in the sand. Then he quietly went on his way.

Moses was out the next day watching the slaves, but this

time he saw two Israelites fighting. "What are you doing, hitting your own Hebrew brother like that?" he demanded.

"And who are you?" one of the brawlers asked Moses. "I suppose you think you are *our* prince and judge! And do you plan to kill me as you did that Egyptian yesterday?"

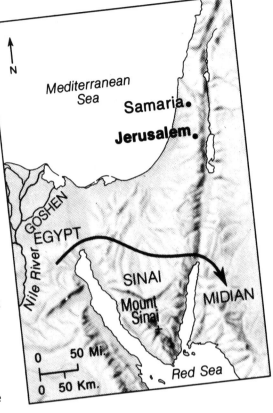

....

Busted! Moses thought there were no witnesses, but he was wrong. Everyone knew about what he had done. While his motives in the killing of the Egyptian were right, the act of murder was wrong. And now Moses was in deep trouble for acting out against an injustice. Many things today are unjust, immoral, or cruel, and, as Christians, we are not to stand by and let these activities continue. But we must be sure to act in a way that God wants and that follows his moral teachings. Anger or sympathy may spur us to action, but we must be sure that action is consistent with God's purposes.

....

Fear struck Moses, who soon took it on the lam. He left Egypt and headed for the land of Midian, which was located in part of modern-day Saudi Arabia, east of the Gulf of 'Aqaba.

In order to get an idea of what that trip must have been like, imagine yourself in Death Valley, California. You don't have a car, motorcycle, or even a bicycle, and there are no truck stops along the way to grab a Coke and a burger. You only have as much food, water, and supplies as you can carry. Now start walking! And don't stop until you reach Las Vegas, Nevada. Not an easy trip, is it? But that is what Moses endured to escape from his death sentence.

Once Moses reached the land of Midian, he came to live with Jethro (another name for him was Reuel), a priest of that area. Moses stayed there for forty years, tending sheep and raising a family. God used those years of watching sheep to help train Moses to be a shepherd to Israel.

....

Training is important for everyone. Police officers, firefighters, salespeople, and even clowns need to be trained before they can do their jobs. Athletes need to train before they can compete in games or tournaments. Training usually isn't a lot of fun, but no one could do anything correctly without it. Even when you don't know you're training for something, you are in training. For example, having a pet teaches you how to be responsible; playing Super Mario Brothers helps you train to be a plumber (just kidding!). Moses was in a situation where he was in training while he was a shepherd—for a job he didn't know existed, the leader of millions of Hebrews out of Egypt! (We can see how well that training worked in the next reading.) The tasks we do today may not seem challenging or even fun, but we may find ourselves in training for something much more important later. We can ask God to help us get through the boring, thankless jobs because something great could be on the horizon.

....

7 · The Exodus

Has your family ever moved? Far away? If so, then you know all the hassles involved with packing, moving, and unpacking. Things get lost, broken, or thrown away. And your new house takes a while before it seems like a home.

Imagine planning a move not only for your family, but for your whole town. If you live in a large city like Atlanta, Boston, Seattle, or Chicago, you would really have a problem, wouldn't you? Oh, by the way, you also don't have any moving vans or U-Hauls. Only donkeys, cattle, oxen, and carts. And you have to move everyone through a desert, like Death Valley. And what's more, there is an army chasing after you. That sounds like a tall order, right? But this was the job that Moses wound up accepting from God.

Not that Moses didn't try to get out of it. He said he wasn't good enough to deliver the Hebrews from Egypt, the people wouldn't believe him, he had a speech problem, etc. After all, he just went up the mountain to see why a bush was burning but wasn't burning up. But God wouldn't allow any lame excuses. No matter how much Moses protested, he still was going back to Egypt.

....

No matter how good our excuses may seem to us, they are all very silly. Just think: If God wants us to do something, he'll make sure we have the strength to do it and do it well. If our excuses come from fear, we can be assured that God will not let us fail something he wants done. And if our excuses come from humility, feeling we are not worthy to do such a job, then we are most likely ready to do that task. After all, who really is worthy to do God's work?

....

If you've ever read a Bible storybook or have ever seen *The Ten Commandments* with Charlton Heston (that is, Charlton Heston was in the movie, not sitting with you watching it), you know the story of what happens once Moses gets to Egypt. If you don't know what happens or have forgotten, put this book down, grab your Bible, and read Exodus 3–12 right now.

OK, now that we're all up to speed, we can skip to when the Hebrews are getting ready to leave. Somehow, overnight, Moses organized 2 million people and their flocks and herds and got them out of the city of Succoth and into the wilderness, heading toward the Promised Land. They didn't get too far, though, by the time Pharaoh changed his mind and took out after them with his army and chariots. The Israelites had possibly camped at Baal-zephon near the Mediterranean Sea, when Pharaoh caught up with them and had them trapped. It was here that God performed an incredible miracle by parting the sea for the Hebrews so they could escape.

19

....

This was only one of many miracles God would do for his people. Whenever they would face an obstacle, he would be there to bail them out. But don't think that God messed up and had to rescue them from his mistake. Instead, he put them in a position where they needed to trust him for his help and thereby build their faith in him. Things like that still happen today, even though God may not part a sea for us. We could find ourselves following God's instructions, but still in a jam. This doesn't mean it's our fault; it is possible we were put there to learn to trust God even more.

....

Once on the other side of the sea, the Hebrew people rejoiced at the destruction of their enemies and at their salvation. Now they were headed for the land that God had promised them and their ancestors.

8 · The Mountain of God

EXODUS 19–20; 32–33

Three long months of marching came to an end, at least temporarily. The Hebrew slaves, led by Moses and God, stood looking up at Mount Sinai, the mountain of God.

Which mountain the Israelites were looking up at is sort of a mystery to us today, since names of places and mountains have changed since Moses' time. No one is sure of its exact location, but the most likely choice of locations is Jebel Müsa. This mountain is located along a two-and-a-half-mile-long ridge of granite that stretches northwest to southeast in the southern Sinai Peninsula, about forty miles from the Red Sea. Jebel Müsa rests on the southern edge of this ridge. (The next time your youth group is doing a study in Exodus, see if you can't work some of this in. It will impress your youth leader! Really.)

It was on this rather imposing mount that God had settled in the form of fire, so the peak was clouded in smoke. The mountain shook, and God's thunderous voice was heard in the camp. It was here that Moses spoke with God and received the Ten Commandments, which were carved out of the same hard, coarse rock as the mountain.

It was also here that the Israelites lost their faith in God after Moses had been on the mount for forty days.

"Moses is dead! Let's make a god to lead us."

And Aaron, the godly brother of Moses, responded, "OK. Give me your jewelry so I can make one." No protests. No arguments. He just made them what they wanted. The image he crafted was a golden calf, and when he saw how much the Israelites liked it, he even made an altar for it and planned a feast.

When God told Moses what was happening, they both were angry at the people. Moses came down from the mount, threw the Ten Commandments to the ground, and destroyed the gold calf.

....

We are forced to wonder, Were the Israelites following God or Moses? When Moses left them and did not return soon, the people felt abandoned and afraid. So they made a false god to take his place, without even thinking that the God of Moses was there to hear their fears. Today, too, we might make the same mistake the Israelites did. Strong leaders in churches are wonderful, and most churches would like to have them. But sometimes people get so wrapped up in following a leader that they forget he is there to help them follow God. If he left that church, would its members still be able to praise and worship God, or would they feel lost and afraid since their leader was no longer there for them? We must always make sure the one we are really following is God.

....

At the foot of Mount Sinai is also where two of the most sacred items in the Bible were built: the Tabernacle and the Ark of the Covenant. The Tabernacle was the traveling tent that God would use to dwell among the people. The Ark was a gold-covered box that was built to hold the Ten Commandments. Its golden lid was called the Mercy Seat. Once a year, on the Day of Atonement, blood was sprinkled on the Mercy Seat to purify the people from their sins.

Once all of the worship items were finished, the people were led across the wilderness by God, moving when God's cloud moved and resting when God's cloud rested on the Tabernacle. They traveled this way to the border of the Promised Land.

....

God is still leading us today, though with nothing so showy as a cloud. Today the Holy Spirit is inside every believer, giving us direction and help when we need it. God's leading may not be visible, but it is real. And it is better now because we don't need someone to talk to God for us, like the Israelites needed Moses and the high priest. We can come right into the presence of God because of what Jesus did.

....

9 · **Two Bears and Ten Chickens**

NUMBERS 13:1–14:45

Moses addressed a group of twelve men, each the leader of one of the tribes of Israel. They all looked very serious—and very expectant.

Why has Moses summoned us? one of the Israelites wondered.

"Men," Moses started, "God has a very special mission for you. As you know, we are headed into the Promised Land, a land flowing with milk and honey. You twelve represent your tribes and are to spy out the land."

Moses gave them further details before they set out. "Go northward into the hill country of the Negeb, and see what the land is like; see also what the people are like who live there, whether they are strong or weak, many or few; and whether the land is fertile or not; and what cities there are, and whether they are villages or are fortified; whether the land is rich or poor, and whether there are many trees. Don't be afraid, and bring back some samples of the crops you see."

With those orders, they set out from Kadesh, near the southern border of the Promised Land, and headed north to see what lay ahead for their nation.

As they journeyed—north to the city of Hebron, then along the Jordan River, up to near the Sea of Galilee, then west to Rehob, on the Mediterranean, which was where the northernmost border of Israel was to be—they were amazed. What they saw was incredible! At one location, they cut off a cluster of grapes so large that two men had to carry it back. For the land was much different then than it is now. What is mostly rough desert now was then rich, lush forests and fertile plains.

They had forty days to explore this incredible land, and then they went back to Kadesh to check in with Moses. When they returned, the spies reported, "Hey, Moses! You won't believe what we saw! Let's get everyone moving and hurry up and take over the land! We can't wait!"

Well, not *all* the spies said this—only two, Joshua and Caleb. They trusted God and his ability to help them conquer the people in Canaan.

But the other ten spies had a different story to tell. "We arrived in the land you sent us to see, and it is indeed a magnificent country—a land 'flowing with milk and honey.' Here is some fruit we have brought as proof. But the people living there are powerful, and their cities are fortified and very large; and what's more, we saw Anakim giants there! The Amalekites live in the south, while in the hill country there are the Hittites, Jebusites, and Amorites; down along the coast of the Mediterranean Sea and in the Jordan River valley are the Canaanites."

When Joshua and Caleb disagreed with them and said victory would be easy, the ten answered, "Not against people as strong as they are! They would crush us!"

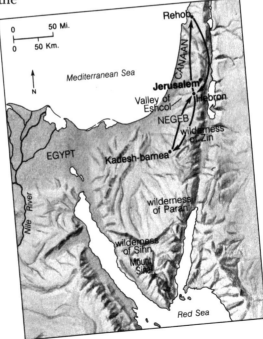

25

....

Who do we listen to? Those who are afraid to trust God or those who will go wherever God leads and try whatever God tells them? If we are honest, the answer, more often than not, would probably be those who are afraid. It is quite easy to get wrapped up in the here and now and forget what God has done for us in the past. The Israelite spies had forgotten that a few months before their spy mission God had rescued them from four hundred years of slavery and from the attack of the Egyptian army. They forgot that God would help them fight their enemies. Do we do the same?

....

The Hebrew people, unfortunately, listened to the ten pessimists and began crying out, complaining to Moses and Aaron. "You led us out here to die! Forget that— let's go back to Egypt!"

As this mutiny was fomenting in the camp, God spoke to Moses, "How long will these people despise me? Will they *never* believe me? . . . I will disinherit them and destroy them with a plague, and I will make you into a nation far greater and mightier than they are!"

Moses defended the Israelites and got their sentence commuted. Instead, God said, "Not one of the men who has seen my glory and the miracles I did both in Egypt and in the wilderness—and ten times refused to trust me and obey me—shall even see the land I promised to this people's ancestors. . . . Not a single one of you twenty years old and older, who has complained against me, shall enter the Promised Land. Only Caleb . . . and Joshua . . . are permitted to enter it. . . . You must wander in the desert like nomads for forty years. In this way you will pay for your faithlessness."

And so they did.

....

God can keep his promises even when we, his people, disobey him. His work will go on, sometimes in spite of us. When we disobey God or lose faith in him, he can still get by without us, but we are the ones who lose out.

....

10 · **Wandering in the Desert**

NUMBERS 21:1-20

Remember taking a trip to Grandma's house or a cousin's house and how the drive there took an hour? On the way there, our brothers or sisters started fights with us, and we wouldn't listen to our dad when he told us to knock it off. Come on, admit it! Well, imagine if our dad, instead of threatening to pull the car over and make us sorry we didn't listen to him, had said that because we wouldn't obey we would have to spend the next two years driving, taking a roundabout way to Grandma's or cousin Eddy's.

Such a thing did happen to the Israelites. They had disobeyed God at the beginning of the journey to the Promised Land, and God punished them by making them wander in the wilderness for forty years, until all the adults who disobeyed him had died. If they had obeyed, they would have arrived in a couple of months. Now it was thirty-seven years later, and many of the older Israelites were dead, including Aaron.

The Israelites broke camp near Mount Hor, the place of Aaron's death, and headed north up into the southern region of modern Israel. This area was controlled by the Canaanites, and the king of Arad was not thrilled to hear of the Israelites' march toward his land. He launched an attack on the wanderers, capturing some. Then the Israelites vowed to God that if he would help them conquer these people, they would totally wipe out their cities. God agreed, and the Israelite army destroyed the army of Arad and the neighboring towns.

27

From there, Moses led the Israelites back to Mount Hor and then southeast, so they would avoid the land of the Edomites, who would not let Israel travel across their territory. Along the way, the Israelites complained again to Moses. "Why have you brought us out of Egypt to die here in the wilderness? There is nothing to eat here, and nothing to drink, and we hate this insipid manna."

....

Why were these people complaining? They had just won a major victory and had been taken care of by God for close to forty years. They complained that there was no food to eat, then they complained when they ate the manna God provided. God was taking great care of the new nation of Israel; but they wanted steak and Cokes instead of what God was providing for their needs. OK, so we all can't have the best the physical world has to offer. So we have to borrow Mom's Escort instead of driving our own Mustang; so we have to bring a lunch to school instead of getting Pizza Hut to deliver to our cafeteria. We mustn't overlook God's care, expecting lots of really cool stuff. He will give us what we need. We should trust him to do that, and then be thankful when he does.

....

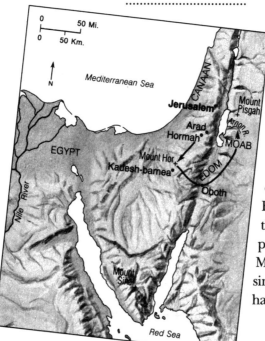

Well, once again God had to discipline his people. Poisonous snakes slithered around the camp, biting and killing many of the Israelites. Begging for their lives, the people came to Moses: "We have sinned, for we have spoken

28

against Jehovah and against you. Pray to him to take away the snakes."

Moses did pray to God, and he answered, but not by taking away the snakes. Rather, he had Moses make a bronze snake and attach it to a pole. Whenever an Israelite was bitten, all he had to do was look at the figure and he would be healed.

....

Why God chose not to take away the snakes is important. This was a foreshadowing of what Christ would come to the world to do. Like the bronze serpent, Jesus would be lifted up upon a pole (a cross), and whoever would look to him for salvation would be saved from death. John 3:14-15 explains, "As Moses in the wilderness lifted up the bronze image of a serpent on a pole, even so I must be lifted up on a pole, so that anyone who believes in me will have eternal life." If we have not yet looked to Jesus for forgiveness, we must realize that the venom of sin is killing us. The only way to save ourselves is to look up to Jesus and ask him to forgive us and to save us.

....

From this camp southeast of Edom, the Israelites moved onward, skirting Edom's border and then heading northeast, along the eastern side of the Dead Sea and then to Mount Pisgah, at the border of the Amorite's land. Here they would launch campaigns over the next three years to take control of most of the land east of the Jordan River, known as the Transjordan.

11 · Preparing to Enter the Promised Land

NUMBERS 32; DEUTERONOMY 33–34; JOSHUA 1

I s this finally it? Are we really going in?" asked one young Israelite. "Soon, soon," answered another, just as anxious as the other.

"Moses just made his speech, and I think I heard one of the leaders saying we'd march into the Promised Land after that."

"We could have been there already if it hadn't been for our fathers and grandfathers," grumbled a tired-looking woman. "If they would have had faith, we wouldn't have had to wander these forty years."

"That won't happen to us!" the first young man said. "I believe Moses. God will fight for us and give us the Promised Land!"

A loud cheer rumbled among those who overheard this conversation.

Moses had climbed Mount Nebo and stood looking west over the Jordan River at the land of Canaan. He could see the lush plains on either side of the river and the rolling Judaean hills far off on the horizon. He had waited many years and endured many hardships, and this was his reward. He stood and beheld the land that held the future for the nation of Israel.

God then spoke to Moses. "There is Naphtali; and there is Ephraim and Manasseh; and across there, Judah, extending to the Mediterranean Sea; there is the Negeb; and the Jordan Valley; and Jericho, the city of palm trees; and Zoar. . . . It is the Promised Land. I promised Abraham, Isaac, and Jacob that I would give it to their descendants. Now you have seen it, but you will not enter it."

Moses knew he wouldn't be able to set foot in this new land. Many years before, Moses disobeyed God by striking a rock to get water when God had only instructed him to speak to it (see Num. 20:1-13), and his punishment was that he would die before the people entered the land. So now he gazed across the plain, ready to go to be with God.

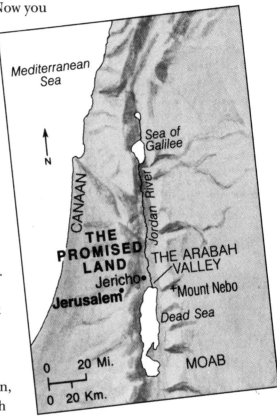

....

Moses was forgiven, but he still could not enter the Promised Land. Why wouldn't God allow him to, considering all he had done for Israel? Because every action has its consequences. In Moses' case, his disobedience led to his ban from the land of Canaan. Moses knew that and accepted the fact. But he did not let it get in the way of his relationship with God. It really was no different than one of us getting caught cheating on a test. Our teacher gives us a zero on the test to punish us for breaking the rules. But later we go back to her and apologize, saying

we understand that it was wrong and we would like to be forgiven. Does she forgive us? Yes. Does she change the zero in the grade book? No way. Punishment helps us to remember the seriousness of what we did so we won't do it again, and it shows other people that they can't get away with the same thing we tried. We may not like being punished for something we did wrong, but we mustn't let our feelings about it keep us apart from our teachers, parents, or especially God.

....

For thirty days, the people of Israel grieved the loss of Moses, the man who rescued them from their enemies and even from God when they disobeyed. Now Joshua was the head honcho. Would he be able to lead as well as Moses had? He must have wondered this. After all, it is hard to follow a legend (just ask Steve Young of the 49ers!).

Soon after Moses died, God spoke to Joshua also, to encourage him. He said, "Be strong and brave, for you will be a successful leader of my people; and they shall conquer all the land I promised to their ancestors. You need only to be strong and courageous and to obey to the letter every law Moses gave you, for if you are careful to obey every one of them, you will be successful in everything you do. . . . Yes, be bold and strong! Banish fear and doubt! For remember, the Lord your God is with you wherever you go."

Joshua responded by telling the people, "In three days we will go across and conquer and live in the land which God has given us!"

....

No doubt, no fear; just confidence in God. Having been placed in a position of more responsibility than he had ever had, Joshua was able to put aside his fear and trust God to take care of him and these few million people. God's promise is for us, too! Imagine God saying to each of us before each scary event in our lives, "Be bold and strong! Banish fear and doubt! For remember, the Lord your God is with you wherever you go."

....

12 · **Spying in Jericho**

JOSHUA 2:1-24

As the Israelites prepared to enter the Promised Land, Joshua ordered two men to spy out the land, especially Jericho, a strong, walled city. The two men set out from Acacia, crossed the Jordan River, and traveled fourteen miles to the city of Jericho. Once they reached Jericho, they had a problem: How would they go unnoticed and get the information they came for?

As they entered the city gate, they noticed, built into the wall, an inn run by Rahab the prostitute. You may be asking how a place like that could be in a wall, right? Many cities had double walls, with about ten or twelve feet between them. This served as double protection from invaders; if they broke through one wall, they still had another to get through. It was on top of these walls that poles were sometimes stretched, and homes were then built on those poles. So while providing a nice view of the countryside, the homes were not ideal locations in times of war.

When the spies saw this hospice, they had a thought. Since men came from the countryside to this inn, two more travelers entering Rahab's wouldn't arouse suspicion. And its location would be perfect for surveying the city and the surrounding area. So the spies entered the inn, pretending to be customers.

But word soon leaked that Israelite spies were in the city. The gates were closed, and a search was begun. The local police went immediately to Rahab's place and demanded that she hand over the men. Rahab was too smart for the police, though. She lied to them, saying that the men had been there but had left just as the gates were closing. Immediately the police left the city and chased after the men, assuming they had taken the road west and were going to cross the Jordan. In reality, Rahab had hidden the men under the flax that was left on the roof to dry.

Once they were safe, Rahab spoke to the spies. "I know perfectly well that your God is going to give my country to you. We are all afraid of you; everyone is terrified if the word *Israel* is even mentioned. . . . Now I beg for this one thing: Swear to me by the sacred name of your God that when Jericho is conquered you will let me live, along with my father and mother, my brothers and sisters, and all their families. This is only fair after the way I have helped you."

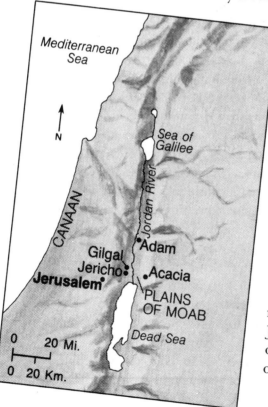

They spies agreed and then climbed down a rope and escaped into the mountains to hide. After three days, the spies returned to Joshua's camp on the west side of the Jordan.

....

God provided help for these two spies from a most unexpected source. We certainly don't expect to see wicked people, such as prostitutes, help the people of God. And while an instance like this is more the exception than the rule, we cannot look down on unbelievers and say to ourselves that they could never be of any help to us and that we don't need them. Had the Israelite spies thought that way, they may have been caught and killed. While it is not advisable to make unbelievers our best friends, we should not avoid them like a plague. It is sinners with whom we are to share Christ's message of salvation, and we cannot do so if we isolate ourselves from them completely. We could also be missing out on some blessings, such as leading a lost person to Christ!

....

In reporting to Joshua, the spies said, "The Lord will certainly give us the entire land, for all the people over there are scared to death of us." There was no doubt in their minds that God was going to help them take the land. The conquest was about to begin.

13 · **The Conquered Land**

JOSHUA 6:1–12:1-24

Once Joshua led the Israelites into Canaan, they faced many years of war. They had to conquer an area of land that stretched about 150 miles north-south and 50 miles east-west. This was a large and difficult job, especially since they were not going to fight just one enemy. Some of the people living there were the Hittites, Jebusites, Anakites, Perizzites, Canaanites, and Amorites, to name a few.

Though this sounds rather intimidating, Joshua had a plan of attack and the promise of God to back him up. First to be conquered was the city of Jericho, a very prominent and secure city across the Jordan River. Once they conquered that city, all other cities would have to be prepared, for if they could take Jericho, no city was safe. After having crossed the Jordan on dry ground and encamping near Jericho (see Josh. 3–7), the Israelites spent a week marching around the city. Finally, on the seventh day of this activity, Jericho's wall came crashing down, and the Israelites were easily able to rout Jericho.

From Jericho, Joshua's army marched eastward to Ai, to establish a firm foothold in the Promised Land. After one unsuccessful battle against this city, the Israelites launched another battle, this time drawing the army away from the city with a diversionary attack. When the armies of Ai and Bethel saw Joshua retreat, they all swarmed after Joshua. Meanwhile, a detachment from Joshua's army had hidden in ambush, and when the city was empty of soldiers, marched in and burned Ai to the ground.

Israel's next campaign was against an alliance of kings from Jerusalem and southward. They were angry at the Gibeonites for making peace with Joshua, so they marched to destroy the Gibeonites. When Joshua heard this, he went to their aid, and so did God. It was

during this battle that Joshua prayed, "Let the sun stand still over Gibeon, and let the moon stand in its place over the valley of Aijalon!" And so they did for twenty-four hours, allowing the Israelites to finish the battle and destroy the alliance. During this same campaign, the Israelites attacked and defeated the cities of Makkedah, Libnah, Lachish, Eglon, Hebron, and Debir. With this campaign, the Israelites controlled the whole southern portion of the Promised Land.

After this stunning victory, an alliance of kings from the northern region of the Promised Land planned an attack at Merom. However, Joshua suddenly attacked the gathered armies and destroyed them. Then, following up, Joshua led his army to each city of the alliance and destroyed it. The

37

Israelites now controlled the north; after seven long years of war, the conquest was basically complete.

....

Are there many practical ways to apply these chapters of Joshua? Sure, especially depending on your interests. The great Confederate general Stonewall Jackson read the book of Joshua and used some of Joshua's battle strategies in his campaigns. Well, if you aren't planning any battles, you can still learn something from these exciting chapters. First, God is in control and all-powerful. Joshua's army wouldn't have been able to win so many victories without the help of God. Second, when we are faithful to God, he will take care of us. When we disobey, like Achan did (see Josh. 7), that is when we see defeats in our life. And third, don't stand against God. Chapter 12 counts the kings that stood in the way of God and his people and lost: thirty-one. So no matter what Bible book we read, there are always truths for us to see—if we are looking.

....

Notice that the conquest was basically complete. Joshua did the big part; he led the major campaigns and routed the major powers. Now it was up to the individual tribes to clear out their inherited land. This proved too difficult for many of the tribes who grew lazy, tired, or comfortable with what they already possessed. The many enemies left in the land would prove troublesome for Israel for hundreds of years to come (see the book of Judges for a taste of the troubles).

....

Are there any pockets of enemies in our lives, enemies that we have grown tired of fighting since we became Christians? And are these enemies causing us trouble as we try to live for God? If so, we need to keep fighting to gain back our lives from sin. A trouble area doesn't mean we aren't saved and are going to hell, but it means that Satan is still able to get at us and possibly tarnish our reputation—or even God's.

....

14 · Samson's Adventures

Roughly three hundred years after Joshua died, the Israelites were still having problems taking possession of the land God had given them.

There were still Jebusites in Jerusalem, Hivites in the north, Moabites east of the Dead Sea, Canaanites near the Sea of Galilee, Midianites in the central region of Canaan, Ammonites east of the Jordan River, and Philistines on the Mediterranean coast and in the lowlands of Judah. And of all these enemies, the Philistines were the most bothersome to Israel.

The Philistines were clearly the dominant force in that region, and they soon controlled much of the central and western portions of Canaan. Naturally, the Israelites didn't want to be ruled by anyone, but the Philistines were more powerful and brought financial rewards to those who dealt with them. But oppression, even profitable oppression, is oppression, so God arranged for a deliverer to come to the aid of Israel. His name was Samson.

But Samson was not without his faults. He had rather uncontrollable urges, especially where Philistine women were concerned. Most of Samson's mistakes were the result of his relationships with women, but God was able to turn these events into victories for Samson and for Israel.

It is possible that we may have problems controlling old habits or wrong behaviors. If so, God can still use us. Problems with our self-discipline do not disqualify us from helping with God's

**work. They just mean that we are human. However, this does
not give us the right to continue in these activities without
working to control them. God desires for us to do our best to
be holy, open to his leadings.**

....

We first see Samson in action when he is getting married to a Philistine girl in the town of Timnah, which was a
few miles from his hometown of Zorah. Having posed a
difficult riddle to the guests, Samson was angered to find
that his new wife had blabbed the answer to them. Since
there was a wager of sixty robes riding on the guessing of
this, Samson went to the town of Ashkelon on the Mediterranean coast, killed thirty Philistines, and then gave their
robes in payment of his wager. Samson then left Timnah
in anger. Later, during the harvest, Samson returned to
Timnah for his wife, but her father had made her marry
Samson's best man. In retaliation, Samson set fire to the
Philistines' crops, thus costing them much money and
food. In revenge, the Philistines burned Samson's wife
and father-in-law to death. Samson in turn killed the
Philistines responsible for his wife's murder.

The Philistines, needless to say, were quite anxious to
get rid of Samson, so they marched to the town of Lehi in
Judah, asking the leaders' help in capturing him. Once
they did so and turned Samson over to them, Samson
broke free from his ropes and killed a thousand Philistines with a donkey's jawbone.

Many years later we see Samson again, and he still is
having problems chasing Philistine women. He was in the
city of Gaza, a key Philistine city on the Mediterranean
Sea. While Samson was with a prostitute, word leaked out
that he was there, and the Philistines planned to capture
him in the morning. But at midnight Samson snuck out a
window and went to the city gate. Instead of quietly sneak-
ing out, Samson picked up the gate, gateposts and all, and
carried them away to Hebron, which was about forty miles

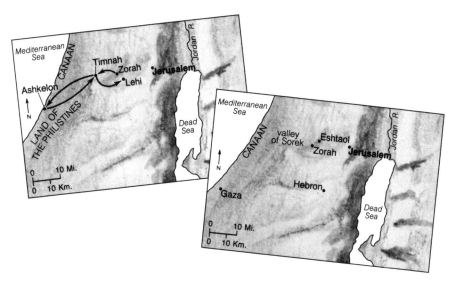

away. Samson must have enjoyed telling the stories of how that gate got to his ruling city.

Our last picture of Samson is tragic. He has been blinded and is in prison in Gaza, the very city he had disgraced earlier with the gate incident. He was caught by a woman named Delilah after she nagged and nagged him to tell her the secret of his strength—his long hair. He did, and she shaved his hair and subdued him for the

Philistine army. But while he was in prison, his hair grew back out and he regained his strength. For his last act, as he was on display in Dagon's temple, he placed his hands on two pillars and prayed, "O Lord Jehovah, remember me again—please strengthen me one more time, so that I may pay back the Philistines for the loss of at least one of my eyes." Then, pushing against the pillars, he finished his prayer, "Let me die with the Philistines." And with that prayer Samson really brought the house down—literally. With that last act he killed even more Philistines than he had before.

41

....

Does physical strength make a person great? Is the biggest, strongest lineman on your school's football team a great

person, or is he just a great football player? Is Mr. Olympia a great man, or is he just muscle-bound? It is what is inside of us that makes us great, not how big our biceps are or how much we can bench press. Samson was an incredibly strong person, but he was not the greatest man around. His spiritual life was marginal, and his problems with women were responsible for many of his actions against the Philistines. If Samson had been a spiritually disciplined person, he might have done far more to rid Israel of the Philistines. Instead, he had to leave that job for a truly great man in God's eyes, King David (see 2 Sam. 8:1). Let's not confuse strength and true greatness.

....

15 · A Flower among Thorns

RUTH 1–4

uring Bible times, when famine struck a land, the people either moved to where there was food, stayed where they were and struggled to feed themselves, or called for Chinese takeout. OK, they didn't order Chinese, but they did have only the other options.

Elimelech, his wife, and his two sons were living in Bethlehem when one of these famines spread over Judah. It was also during this time that the judges ruled Israel, and the nation was somewhere near the bottom of the barrel spiritually. Everyone was doing what he thought was right, and no one was really paying any attention to God (see Judg. 21:25). Since everyone did whatever he wanted, it isn't surprising that Elimelech, hoping to feed himself and his family, packed up his family and moved to the land of Moab, one of Israel's enemies.

While in this land, Elimelech died. That left only the two sons and their mother. Soon the sons married Moabite girls, Ruth and Orpah. But these men died, too, leaving all three women to fend for themselves in a world that was unkind to widows. By this time the famine in Israel had ceased, so Naomi, with her two daughters-in-law, returned to her homeland.

On the trip back, Naomi changed her mind about bringing Ruth and Orpah to Israel. Life would be tough on Naomi, and she thought that these girls would manage better

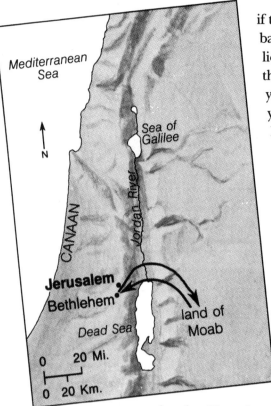

if they were to go back to their families. She said to them, "Why don't you return to your parents' homes instead of coming with me? And may the Lord reward you for your faithfulness to your husbands and to me. And may he bless you with another happy marriage."

The girls argued with her, but Naomi wouldn't hear of it. She had no other sons for them to marry, so she wanted them to go back home to their parents. Orpah finally agreed, and she went back to Moab (where she hosted a very popular daytime talk show).

But Ruth wouldn't hear of such a thing! She answered Naomi, "Don't make me leave you, for I want to go wherever you go and to live wherever you live; your people shall be my people, and your God shall be my God."

....

Ruth here basically converted to Judaism, accepting the people and God of Israel as her own. Naomi must have been some woman! She practically has to force her daughters-in-law to leave her, and even then one won't leave. Something she did made these girls, especially Ruth, want to stay with her and accept her God. We don't have any evidence that Naomi preached to Ruth and Orpah; instead, she was such a faithful Jew that Ruth knew this God was a God to get to know. Do we have that effect on others? Would someone say to us, "Hey! I don't want to leave you because you're so cool! And Jesus must really be alive because I see him in you. How can I meet Jesus myself?" If not, that should be our goal.

....

Once Naomi and Ruth returned to Bethlehem, it was time for the barley harvest—that is, sometime in April or May. These women had no source of income and no food, so Ruth decided to go out and glean the fields. The one she arrived at was owned by a relative of Naomi's, Boaz. Boaz saw her out there, following his reapers and picking up whatever grain was left, and he questioned his foreman about her. He told Boaz that she had returned with Naomi and that she had been hard at work with only a few minutes' break. Boaz was impressed and invited her for a drink of water.

While they were talking—you know, this part gets kind of mushy, so we better skip over some of it. If you like the love-story stuff, why don't you read Ruth 2–4. Let's just say that Ruth and Boaz got married and had a son. This son, as it happened to turn out, was Obed. That name might not mean much to you, but he was King David's grandfather. So Ruth, a woman foreigner, became an ancestor of Jesus.

....

During this time in history, there were a few faithful people, such as Naomi, Ruth, and Boaz. They worshiped God and were kind to others, going the extra mile when they didn't have to. As a result, they were rewarded, both with the company of each other and with a part in bringing the Savior into the world. No matter how bad times seem to be, God's people can always do good and be faithful. Who knows what we could be a part of if we stay open to God?

....

16 · The Ark's Travels

1 SAMUEL 4:1–7:2

Israel and the Philistines were at war, which was nothing new. The Israelites and the Philistines were bitter enemies and fought for many, many years. During one particular battle the Philistines beat Israel. The Israelite leaders didn't know why God let them lose. Then someone thought that if they brought the Ark of the Covenant into battle, they couldn't possibly lose. So they took the Ark from the Tabernacle in Shiloh and brought it to the battlefield near the towns of Ebenezer and Aphek. Much to the surprise of the Israelites, they lost again, this time much worse than before. Not only did many Israelites die, but the Philistine army captured the Ark of God!

How could this have happened? The Israelites trusted God, right? Not exactly. They trusted in the Ark, an object. They treated it like we might treat a rabbit's foot—as a good-luck charm. By having the Ark with them, they figured God would be there and protect them. But they were wrong. God wanted them to pray to him and ask him for help. Instead they broke God's laws concerning the Ark: The Ark was supposed to stay in the Most Holy Place in the Tabernacle, and only the High Priest was supposed to enter the Most Holy Place. Because of their disobedience, God taught the Israelites a lesson and let the Philistines beat them.

But the Ark caused many problems for the Philistines, too. They brought it to the city of Ashdod, where the temple of their false god Dagon was. They put the Ark in with Dagon's idol, possibly to show how the Israelite God was beaten by Dagon's power. But the next day Dagon was knocked over. The Philistines propped him back up, but the next day he fell over again, and this time his head and hands broke off. The Philistines were afraid, so they moved the Ark to another city, Gath. But the people in this city got sick from a plague, and they sent the Ark on to Ekron. The same thing happened to the people at Ekron.

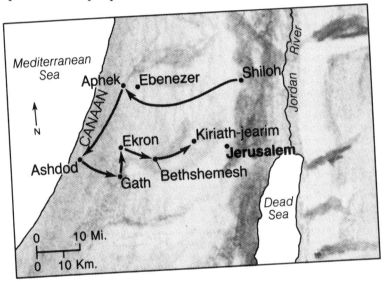

After seven months, the Philistines figured out that they had to get rid of the Ark. So they made golden images of tumors and rats as an offering to God. Then the Ark and the gold images were loaded on a cart that was hitched to some cows. God directed the cows to the town of Beth-shemesh, which was under Israelite control.

You would think that the Israelites would have obeyed God's laws about the Ark now that they had it back, wouldn't you? But they didn't. Seventy men of Beth-shemesh died because they looked inside the Ark, something God told them never to do. So the people of Beth-shemesh begged the people of Kiriath-jearim to take the Ark and keep it safe, and the Ark remained in Kiriath-jearim for twenty years.

We don't have the Ark today, but we do have the Bible, God's Word to us. And, like the Israelites, we sometimes treat the Bible like a good-luck charm. We do this when we get a nice, fancy-looking Bible and place it on our desk or our dresser and never read it. We think that because we have a cool Bible, God will teach us something. Remember, the Bible is not the Ark—God *wants* us to open it and learn!

17 · **David and Goliath**

1 SAMUEL 17

How would you like to be anointed king of a whole nation? Sounds pretty good, huh? But lets say that you can't be king until the current king dies. And that in the meantime you have to work part-time for the king and still look after your dad's sheep. Does it sound as exciting now? And to top it off, you have to run errands for your seven older brothers who are in the army and at the front lines of a battle. These are some of the trials David had to endure before he could actually become king of Israel.

On one particular day David left Bethlehem with some food for his brothers and made the fifteen-mile trip westward to the valley of Elah, where the Israelite army was camped. When he got there and was talking with his brothers, he looked out across the valley. On his side, on the ridge, was the Israelite army, weapons in hand. On the opposite ridge was the Philistine army, looking much more confident than the Israelites. Even though David was young, he understood why the armies faced each other across this valley. Whoever made the first attack would have to rush down one steep hill and then across an open field to run up another steep hill. The defending army would then have an easy time picking off the soldiers as they made their way across the open plain and struggled uphill. Since no army wanted to be sitting ducks (or climbing ducks), they had managed to maintain a standoff for forty days.

On this day, as had happened twice a day, every day, a giant stepped out from the Philistine lines. He stood there and yelled insults and curses at the Israelites. For forty days Goliath had been shouting the same thing across the battlefield: "Do you need a whole army to settle this? I will represent the Philistines, and you choose someone to represent you, and we will settle this in single combat! If your man is able to kill me, then we will be your slaves. But if I kill him, then you must be our slaves! . . . Send me a man who will fight with me!" (We assume the writer of this book edited out the really nasty, insulting stuff.)

Because of the aforementioned dilemma, such a tactic was common among armies of this time. Each side would select a champion, and these two men would engage in hand-to-hand combat. Whoever won the fight won the battle for his side, and then everyone could go home. Or, in this case, the losers would have to submit to being the winning side's slaves. And since no one in the Israelite army was over nine feet tall, like Goliath was, the Philistines were feeling pretty confident they'd be chalking one up in the win column.

Well, young David couldn't stand to hear Israel and her God insulted, so he volunteered to go out and fight the giant. At first, no one took him seriously since he was just a kid and Goliath was such a huge monster. But David said that he had to fight off lions and bears while he was shepherding, and he wrapped up his argument with, "The Lord who saved me from the claws and teeth of the lion and the bear will save me from this Philistine!" After he heard all of this, King Saul reluctantly agreed, and he sent David out to fight. Armed only with a shepherd's staff, a slingshot, and five stones, David headed out across the plain toward Goliath.

"Am I a dog that you come at me with a stick?" Goliath shouted to David, cursing him. Goliath must have felt a little

50

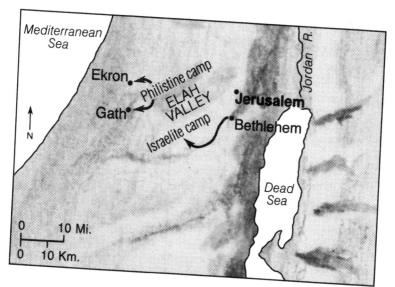

insulted when he saw
a kid come out to fight him. "Come over here and I'll give
your flesh to the birds and wild animals."

David answered Goliath, correcting him about the weapons he carried. "You come to me with a sword and a spear,
but I come to you in the name of the Lord of the armies of
heaven and of Israel—the very God whom you have defied.
Today the Lord will conquer you, and I will kill you and cut
off your head; and then I will give the dead bodies of *your*
men to the birds and wild animals, and the whole world will
know that there is a God in Israel!"

As they approached each other for battle, David pulled
out his sling and threw a stone, which sank into Goliath's
forehead. When Goliath hit the ground, David rushed
over to him, pulled Goliath's own sword, and cut his head
off. When the Philistine army saw the unexpected outcome of the battle, they took off running. The Israelites
shouted for joy and chased the Philistines across the countryside, all the way to the Philistine cities of Ekron and
Gath.

So David and God won a major victory.

....

Fear is an excellent excuse for not doing something. It stops us from trying out for athletic teams, from answering a question in class, from asking out that cute guy or girl who sits next to us in math. But we also miss out on great things because fear controls us: We don't become the star running back or soccer player, we don't answer the question in class and earn brownie points with the teacher, and we never go out with that cute guy/girl in our math class. In the spiritual realm, fear stops us from witnessing to our friends, from taking more responsibilities in church, maybe even from accepting Christ as Savior. Do we really want to live in fear and not see our friends become Christians, not do more to help others in church, not accept the best gift in the whole world? Of course not! We need to confront the Goliaths in our life. For David, Goliath was his Goliath. David put aside his fear and trusted God to protect him and give him the victory. We can be confident that God will be there to help us, for the Bible reminds us, "Is anything too hard for God?" (Gen. 18:14).

....

18 · **Hide and Seek**

1 SAMUEL 22–24

Jealousy. Power struggles. Betrayals. Murder. Do these sound like some of the story lines on a soap opera? They could be, but actually those words are describing the story of two important men in the Bible: King Saul and David.

Saul was the king, and he was paranoid, thinking David was trying to steal the throne. The prophet Samuel anointed David to be king, but David was unwilling to take the crown before Saul died. Had Saul been able to get that through his head, they both could have avoided years of aggravation. But such was not the case.

Instead, David became something of a Bible-times Robin Hood, leading a band of four hundred ruffians and low-lifes through the wilderness, attacking the enemy whenever possible. His Sherwood Forest was the deserts and hills of Israel, and his headquarters was in a cave near Adullam, a town close to the land of the Philistines. Here David hid out, avoiding fighting with Saul ("God's anointed" as David called him) and raiding God's enemies, the Philistines. One such raid occurred in the Israelite town of Keilah, a few miles south of David's cave. The Philistines were stealing the grain from the town's threshing floors, so David and his men went to the city's aid.

When King Saul heard of this, he was overjoyed, not because David had helped his subjects, but because David was in a walled city where he could capture him. So he began to march his army from Gibeah to kill David.

David, in the meantime, had heard of Saul's plans, and he asked the Lord what to do. God told David that Saul was really coming and that the people of the city he just saved would turn him in to Saul.

....

People have a funny way of showing their gratitude, don't they? David saved them from the Philistines, so naturally they decide to thank him by handing him over to the man who wants him dead. Some thanks! But David probably would have rescued them again if they needed it, because they were his people and because God's enemies couldn't be allowed to win. Likewise, when we have the opportunity to do good, we shouldn't be concerned about being rewarded or even thanked. We should do good because God wants us to help others (like the Good Samaritan) and because God's enemies cannot be allowed to win!

....

Well, David wasn't going to sit around and be captured, so he and his six hundred men (two hundred more joined him, possibly from Keilah) fled south to the wilderness and hid in a cave near Horesh. Saul found out again and came after David, who went farther south in the wilderness, near Maon.

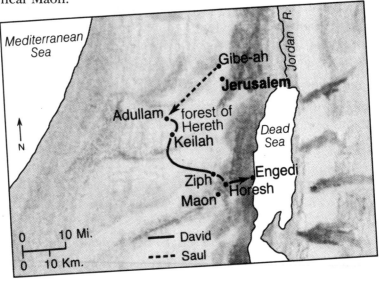

19 · **The Battle of Gilboah**

1 SAMUEL 29–31

If ever Saul needed David on his side, it was now. He was entering what was to be his last battle, and he needed good, experienced men to aid him in his fight against the Philistines. But, unfortunately for Saul, he had continued to hunt David and would not accept David's offers of friendship; thus the man who had slain tens of thousands of enemies was sidelined. Not only was he sidelined, he was on the wrong team's sidelines!

You see, David had spent the last several years living with the Philistines, and he and his men naturally accompanied the Philistines in battle. But the battle to come was to be unusual, for David would have to fight his brothers and King Saul. And since David had promised never to hurt God's anointed, he was in a pickle.

But the Philistine leaders understood the situation. They marched to the Philistine king Achish and demanded, "Send them back! They aren't going into battle with us—they'll turn against us. Is there any better way for him to reconcile himself with his master than by turning against us in the battle?" So King Achish sent for David and told him to leave Aphek and go back home to Ziklag.

....

What would David have done if he did go into battle against Saul and Jonathan, his best friend? Could he really have fought his fellow Israelites? Or would he have turned against the Philistines who had accepted him, and allied himself with Saul? Fortunately for David, God spared him this decision.

Saul's troops came and pinned David in, leaving no escape. Then, on the verge of battle, Saul received a mes. The Philistines were raiding Israelite land again. Saul relu tantly had to give up on David and take care of the larger enemy. Once King Saul's army left, David and his men to off and hid in the caves of Engedi, on the western coast o the Dead Sea.

....

God was indeed watching over David. He aided David when David prayed to him, and he arranged for other matters to distract Saul from his hunt. God was with David as he roame throughout the deserts, hills, and caves all over Canaan. Actually, David had little to worry about, since God promised him that he would be king of Israel. God's plans can't be messed up by anyone—not by kings, politicians, laborers, or criminals. King Saul would not be able to kill David, even though Saul was a skilled military man. His skill never entered into the picture; God's plans made his skill irrelevant. We mustn't worry too much if it seems God is losing in this world. His plans are secure, and ultimately no one will be able to defeat God (or us!).

....

**The Philistines sent him far away from the battlefield so there
would be no question of whose side David would fight for.
When it seems that we are between a rock and a hard place,
God is there, watching out for us and helping us out of jams.**

....

While David was away with the Philistine army, a band
of Amalekite raiders came up from the south and attacked
Ziklag, David's town, burned it down, and took away all the
people. After consulting God, David and his men chased
after the raiders, eventually catching them and retrieving
everything that had been stolen.

Meanwhile, Saul was not having such a successful time.
The Philistines had attacked Israel much farther north than
expected. They had a fairly easy march up the flatlands near
the Mediterranean
coast, and the battle
would go much
better for them if
they attacked the
weaker and more-
accessible north-
ern area rather
than the mountain-
ous midsection of
Israel. Thus Saul
had to mobilize
his army, which
was near Bethel
in the south
central part of
Israel, and
march through
the rough,
mountainy
land up to
Shunem.

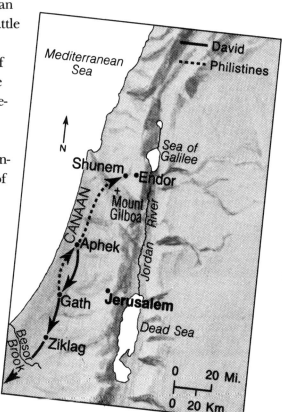

The battle began at Jezreel, which was just south of Shunem, and the Israelites fled the battlefield to Mount Gilboah. It was here that Israel's army was "slaughtered wholesale." Saul's sons were killed, and Saul was gravely wounded by Philistine archers. Not wanting to be tortured by the enemy, Saul fell on his sword and committed suicide. Thus ended his reign of forty-two years.

....

Saul reigned for a long time, but he rarely had peace of mind. When he was young, he didn't want to become king. When he was king, he couldn't fully trust God and follow him. Then after he had pushed God too far and God chose another to be king after him, Saul became paranoid and wasted much of his reign chasing David. Saul was God's anointed, as David called him many times, yet he rejected the peace that God's anointing can bring. God is ready and willing to calm us and bring us peace with him, with our enemies, and with ourselves, if we can fully put our trust and faith in him. This will take a lot of work and practice, but God's peace is better than any peace worldly things can give us (see John 14:27).

....

20 · **David Conquers Everyone**

1 CHRONICLES 18:1-17

I n this one chapter of the Bible we see the culmination of about five hundred years' work. Back when Moses led the Israelites out of Egypt, God promised them a "land flowing with milk and honey," which was, for obvious reasons, called the Promised Land. The only problem was that only Moses, Joshua, and Caleb really seemed to want to fight for the land; the other leaders fell short of their duty and never fully conquered the territory God promised them. During the time of the judges, Israel not only didn't conquer much land but it lost some to people like the Philistines and Moabites, who oppressed Israel for long stretches of time. God would send a leader to rescue them, and then a few years after that leader's death, they would be back in trouble again. This cycle continued until Israel asked for a king.

....

Even though God promised this land to the Israelites, they had to physically conquer it. The land was already theirs as far as God was concerned, but they did not trust him enough to fight for it. No doubt the Israelites saw how strong the enemies were, and they became afraid and forgot that an invisible God was there fighting for them. We, too, can easily forget that God is with us because we can't actually see him. We know things we see are real, like bullies and tests, and we're afraid that if we can't see it, it isn't there. So we forget that God is there to help us. We need to constantly remind ourselves that God is there beside us, able to jump to our aid when we ask him.

....

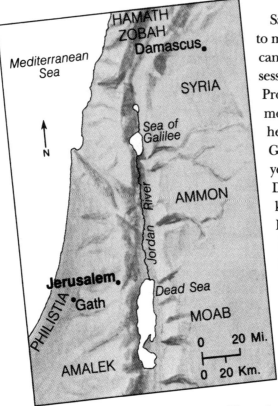

Saul was unable to make any significant gains in possessing the entire Promised Land, mostly because he disobeyed God and spent years chasing David instead of killing enemies. King David, however, was finally able to get the job done and take the land God had promised hundreds of years before.

Though it only takes us a couple of minutes to read the account of David's victories and expansion of Israel, it really took several years to accomplish. In fact, many of the events going on in the first twelve chapters of 2 Samuel were happening during the time that David was conquering these lands.

After becoming king of Israel, David captured the city of Jerusalem and made it his headquarters. After that, he defeated the biggest pain in his backside, the Philistines, who lived along the Mediterranean coast. He took over their land, except for one small patch of territory. Once that was taken care of, David focused on the rest of the Promised Land. The Moabites east of the Dead Sea were conquered. So were the Amalekites, who lived south of Israel. The Ammonites east of the Jordan River were crushed, too. Also, David went into Syria and took over their capital city of Damascus and then extended his control up to Tadmor, a city in the middle of modern-day Syria. In all, David conquered just about all of the land promised Israel, and then more besides. If you look at the map here, David controlled most of this land plus land stretching farther south to the Gulf of 'Aqaba and north, well into Syria.

....

When we hear of all the fighting in the Middle East, the issue of the Promised Land is central to the disputes. If we look at a modern map or globe, we can see that parts of Syria, Lebanon, and Jordan lie in areas that God promised to Israel thirty-five hundred years ago and were taken over by David. Israel feels that this land belongs to them, and they want it. Other nations, such as Iraq, Iran, and Egypt, have ancestors who once possessed or took over the Promised Land; and they are also friends and Arab brothers with the nations that now have land there. And then there are the Palestinians, who claim that the present nation of Israel should be their homeland, not the Jews'. Considering all of these relation-ships and how many centuries the conflicts have lasted, any long-term peace seems improbable. Only when God brings the new earth will there be lasting peace, and territorial dis-putes won't matter: All of God's people will share paradise.

....

21 · **Absalom's Rebellion**

2 Samuel 15–18

There is an old saying that the person who wants power most is the least qualified to have it. There can be a lot of truth to that. This saying definitely applies to one of David's sons: Absalom. Absalom was one of those brothers you'd never want to have. He was good-looking, popular, and mean! After Absalom found out his sister Tamar had been raped by their half-brother Amnon, he plotted for two years and eventually killed Amnon. While what Amnon did was horrible, Absalom's plotting and cold-blooded murder were no better. It wouldn't be hard to believe that when he was young he would start fights with his brothers and pull the legs off daddy longlegs.

Nine years had passed since he killed his brother, and he was again in Jerusalem after having been banished for three years. He spent his first couple of years back in Jerusalem waiting to see his father, who wouldn't talk to him. Absalom could only take so much of this treatment before he plotted to get even with his dear ol' dad.

....

Most families aren't like we see on the reruns on "Nick at Nite." Brothers and sisters really do have problems with each other, and children can seriously rebel against their family. Anger and unforgiveness can destroy a person and a family. It isn't always easy, but talking to and forgiving each other is the best way to make a peaceful room (if we have to share a bedroom) or house. If anger festers, it will lead to revenge, which will make the other person angry, and he'll fester and take revenge, and

so on. And while we might not behave like Absalom, why take the chance that a brother or sister might?!

....

Setting up a chair by the main gate of Jerusalem (the gate was a spot where people took care of business dealings), Absalom would call over those who had cases to bring before King David. "I can see that you are right in this matter," he would tell these people, "it's unfortunate that the king doesn't have anyone to assist him in hearing these cases. I surely wish I were the judge; then anyone with a lawsuit could come to me, and I would give him justice!" And when these people would try to bow to him in respect, Absalom would just shake their hand like he was one of them. Needless to say, he became very popular.

So popular, in fact, that he decided to take over the kingdom from David. Returning to his hometown and former capital of Israel, Absalom had himself declared king. When David learned what had happened, he ordered his troops to leave Jerusalem, "If we get out of the city before he arrives, both we and the city of Jerusalem will be saved." So fearing

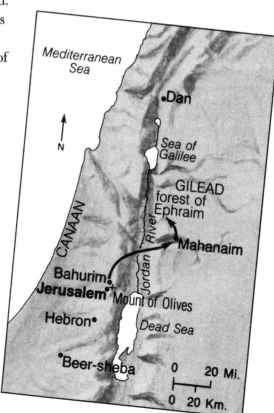

63

for the safety of God's city, David fled across the Jordan River to the town of Mahanaim. (Mahanaim, meaning "God's territory," was the town where angels greeted Jacob as he prepared to meet his brother, who was pretty ticked at him the last time they saw each other. The angels affirmed to Jacob that God was with him, and David must have had this in mind when he approached this region. See Gen. 32 for this story.)

Absalom gathered Israel's army and chased David, eventually engaging in battle north of Mahanaim in the forest of Ephraim. This group led by young Absalom was no match for David's experienced generals, and the rebellion was soon crushed. Absalom himself fled from the scene, only to get his long, beautiful hair tangled in a tree, leaving him hanging there. Joab, commander of David's army, found Absalom dangling by his hair, and he and his men killed Absalom.

....

Absalom did some despicable things in his time, and he died in disgrace. It's easy to say he had it coming, and he may well have. But each of us is no better in God's sight. James tells us that if we have broken one of God's laws, we have broken them all and are worthy of death (see James 2:10). But forgiveness is available to us if we trust in Christ to take away our sins. If you haven't asked Christ to forgive you, you can do so and be free from sin and have eternal life. Talk to a parent, youth leader, or pastor if you have any questions or want someone to pray with you.

....

22 · The Temple

Ｔhe Lord my God has given Israel peace on every side; I have no foreign enemies or internal rebellions. So I am planning to build a Temple for the Lord my God, just as he instructed my father that I should do." Solomon had been king of Israel now for four years, and it was now time to begin work on the Temple, the place where God's presence could stay with Israel. Solomon, seeking labor and building materials, continued his message to Hiram of Tyre: "Now please assist me with this project. Send your woodsmen to the mountains of Lebanon to cut cedar timber for me, and I will send my men to work beside them, and I will pay your men whatever wages you ask; for as you know, no one in Israel can cut timber like you Sidonians!"

King Hiram liked Solomon's message (especially that last bit of flattery), and he agreed to cut timber for the Temple. "My men will bring the logs from the Lebanon mountains to the Mediterranean Sea and build them into rafts. We will float them along the coast to wherever you need them; then we will break the rafts apart and deliver the timber to you."

With timber coming from Sidon (modern Lebanon, north of Israel, along the Mediterranean coast), and laborers coming from Israel, Sidon, and Gebal (farther north along the Mediterranean), the Temple was on its way to becoming a reality. Solomon arranged to have almost two

hundred thousand laborers and stonecutters working on
the Temple. The stonework was done at the quarries and
the timber cut outside Jerusalem, so that the Temple was
put together without the sound of a hammer—the pieces
of stone and wood must have fit like an enormous, and
very heavy, jigsaw puzzle!

....

**Does anything in this description strike you as odd? Where
did the materials come from? And who helped build the
Temple? Nonbelievers, that's who! David and Solomon both
recognized who the best workers were, and they made sure
these people did their finest work in building God's home.
Solomon also offered to pay Hiram anything he felt was
appropriate; he didn't try to talk Hiram into donating the
materials and labor time, hoping to convince him he'd find
favor with God by doing so. When we have something that
needs to be done, it isn't necessary that Christians are the
ones to do the work. It is nice to give other Christians our
business to help them out, but it isn't necessary. God accepts
the work of non-Christians, too. Whether it is looking for
someone to build a church or someone to tutor us in chemis-
try, we should seek out the person with the best qualifica-
tions. And if that person isn't a Christian, maybe the time
spent working for us will show that person something of
what Christians are like, and hopefully something of what
God is like.**

....

The Temple took seven years to complete, and when it
was finished, it was one the most beautiful buildings in the
world. The floors were cedar, and the walls were engraved
and covered with gold. If you could enter the Holy Place,
you'd see at the other end of the room a large curtain col-
ored purple, red, and blue, with gold embroidery; this separated the Holy Place from the Most Holy Place, where
the Ark of the Covenant was kept. In this room were two
gold-covered cherubim, with each one's wings stretching
from one wall to the other to cover the Ark. The walls
were covered with gold, as was the Ark. It might be hard
to imagine this as being attractive; with all that gold, the
Temple could have been overwhelming. But the brilliance

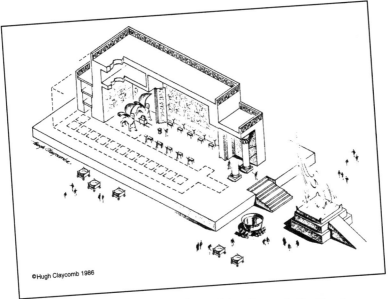

©Hugh Claycomb 1986

of the gold reflected God's glory and purity. If you ever visit a cathedral, you might be able to get some idea of the grand scale of the building and of how the gold and statues contributed to the sense of awe one would have felt upon entering the Temple.

The outside of the Temple was impressive, too. Two bronze pillars stood at the entrance to the Temple. A huge bronze tank stood in front of the whole Temple building; it rested on twelve bronze bulls and was for the priests to wash in before accepting sacrifices. A gold altar was directly in front of the Temple and was the place where the sacrifices were made. These items must have glistened in the bright sunlight. And don't think people couldn't see the Temple or these items. The Temple was built on the highest point in Jerusalem, with the Most Holy Place being over the spot where Abraham almost sacrificed Isaac (see Gen. 22) and where David had sacrificed to stop a plague (Araunah's threshing floor; see 2 Sam. 24).

If you went to Jerusalem tomorrow, you couldn't see

67

the Temple. Nebuchadnezzar destroyed it in 586 B.C. Nor could you see the Temple that Zerubbabel built after the Exile; the Romans destroyed that in A.D. 70. What is standing where the Temple used to be is the Mosque of Omar, or the Dome of the Rock, the second most holy site for Muslims (Mecca in Saudi Arabia is the first).

23 · Israel Splits

Everything had been going pretty well for Israel, that is, up to now. David had conquered Israel's enemies; Solomon had made Israel incredibly rich; and the Temple was built. But there was a problem: Solomon had turned away from God and was worshiping other gods.

To punish Solomon for his false worship, God appointed Jeroboam, a supervisor of laborers, to be king of Israel. The prophet Ahijah told Jeroboam, "The Lord God of Israel says, 'I will tear the kingdom from the hand of Solomon and give ten of the tribes to you! . . . I will not take the kingdom from him now, however; for the sake of my servant David, my chosen one who obeyed my commandments, I will let Solomon reign for the rest of his life'" (1 Kings 11:31, 34).

....

Notice that even though Solomon was a bonehead for disobeying God, God still kept his promise to keep a son of David on the throne of Israel forever. The only catch was that David's line would only rule over two tribes, not all twelve. Solomon didn't negate the promise; he just limited the blessings God was able to give to his people. When we make a mistake or disobey him, God won't change his mind and break his promise to save us. Instead, our mistake can cost us some good things from God, but not our salvation. Be thankful that God is willing to forgive us boneheads.

....

Somehow Solomon found out about Jeroboam's claim to the throne and tried to kill Jeroboam, who escaped to Egypt.

When Solomon died, his son Rehoboam became king, and Jeroboam returned.

At his inauguration, Rehoboam heard the crowd, led on by Jeroboam, say, "Your father was a hard master. We don't want you as our king unless you promise to treat us better than he did."

Rehoboam had to think about treating his subjects nicely, so he said he would answer them in three days. During those days, he asked for advice.

"King Rehoboam, if you treat these people decently and answer them kindly, they'll follow you all their lives," his father's advisors told him.

But Rehoboam didn't like this advice, so he asked his buddies what they thought. "Hey, man! You're the king! You can do whatever you want. Tell them that if they thought your father was hard, they ain't seen nothin' yet." This sounded a lot more fun to the new king, and that was his answer to the crowd.

Now if you were part of this crowd and you heard that your contribution to the king's coffers was going to be worse than the taxes before and that you'd be beaten, not with whips, but with scorpions, you'd rebel, right? That's exactly what the crowd did. They shouted, "Let's go home! Let Rehoboam be king of his own family!" And they all marched off north to their homes. So the ten northern tribes seceded from Israel's union, proclaiming Jeroboam as their king, and Rehoboam was left king over Judah and the tiny tribe of Benjamin.

....

It's important to listen to people who have more experience than we do. Their advice may not seem fun or be what we want to do, but generally older, experienced people have learned from their mistakes, the same mistakes we might make if we don't heed their warnings. Clearly Rehoboam didn't like his father's advisors (probably old men), and his decision cost him much of his kingdom. We'd be surprised at the wisdom older people can impart to us. (Also, they tell some great stories!)

....

Once Jeroboam and the northern tribes broke off from Rehoboam, they became their own nation, taking the name *Israel* for themselves (also called the *Northern Kingdom*). So anytime after this point in the Bible, the name *Israel* can either mean the Northern Kingdom or the whole nation (both halves). Israel owned everything north and east of the Dead Sea (area on map with horizontal lines), all the way up past the Sea of Galilee to the border with Syria. Rehoboam's kingdom became known as Judah after its larger tribe (also called the *Southern Kingdom*), and its territory stretched from west of the Dead Sea down south to one of the gulfs of the Red Sea (everything covered by vertical lines). The kingdoms would be divided like this until they were both destroyed many years later.

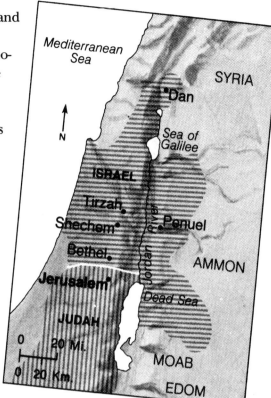

24 · **Elijah Hides from Ahab**

1 KINGS 17

How would you like to have this as a job: to talk to people who don't want to listen about things they don't want to hear and that they won't do anyway. If this sounds like the job for you, you may want to look into being a prophet to an evil kingdom. But if you're thinking about a career with job security, forget it!

Look at Elijah, for example. The first time we see him at work, he is addressing Ahab, the wicked king of Israel, the Northern Kingdom. Elijah proclaimed, "As surely as the Lord God of Israel lives—the God whom I worship and serve—there won't be any dew or rain for several years until I say the word!"

We don't know what Ahab's exact response was, but we do get the idea that he was not happy. We can surmise this by God's command to Elijah: "Go to the east and hide by Cherith Brook at a place east of where it enters the Jordan River. Drink from the brook and eat what the ravens bring you, for I have commanded them to feed you." Had Ahab chosen to listen to Elijah and repent, Elijah wouldn't have been running for his life, and God probably would have cancelled, or at least shortened, the drought.

....

If we've ever tried to tell other people about what Christ has done for us, or how he can help someone else, we've probably gotten the same reception that Elijah received. Our lives might not have been in jeopardy, but we were laughed at, mocked, or treated like fanatics. But that's the way it is when we share

God's message with others: They will hurt us, make fun of us, or ignore us—not because of us, but because of the message we bring. If we are treated badly by others for telling them about God, God will be pleased because we are doing what we should. If others won't accept the message, that is not our responsibility. We are to give them the message; God will take care of the rest.

....

Elijah, being a faithful guy, did what God said, and he pitched his tent by the brook in the wilderness, trusting unclean scavengers for his dinners. This brook was still in Ahab's kingdom, but it was remote enough to ensure that no one was going to go looking for him there. But soon the brook dried up, placing Elijah in a rough spot. But God knew the problem, so he said to Elijah: "Go and live in the village of Zarephath, near the city of Sidon. There is a widow there who will feed you."

But when Elijah got to Zarephath and met the widow, she said she only had enough food left for one meal, then she and her son would die from hunger. A lesser person would have been ticked at God for making him travel over seventy miles through the wilderness into a town of unbelievers just to starve. But Elijah wasn't sent there to be

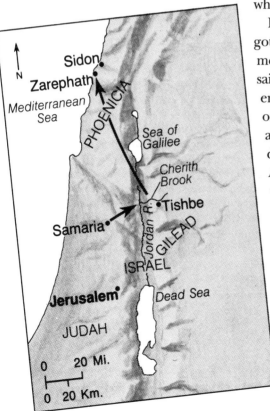

73

served; he came there to serve the widow. He told her that as long as they needed the oil and flour, it would last—the containers would never empty!

Elijah was also there to save a life, the life of the widow's son. Her son got sick and died one day, and she blamed Elijah, asking him if her son died to pay for her sins. This whole situation troubled Elijah, so he carried the boy upstairs to his room, laid him on the bed, and stretched himself on top of the boy's body three times, praying to God to let the child's spirit return. God heard Elijah, and he brought the boy back to life. When the woman saw this, she was ecstatic. Later she told him, "Now I know for sure that you are a prophet, and that whatever you say is from the Lord!" For three years Elijah stayed in this town, being a faithful witness for God.

....

Why didn't Elijah perform these miracles in Israel instead of the Phoenician town of Zarephath? It seems that the answer is that Israel wouldn't listen to him and recognize the miracles as from God. Jesus would later use this as an example of how prophets are not welcome in their own towns. Elijah was from Israel, but he had to go to a foreign land to be listened to. Jesus himself was rejected in Nazareth and Capernaum, his hometowns. We, too, may find that no one in our church or youth group will listen when we have valuable things to say that the Lord has shown us. We shouldn't be afraid to tell other people—they may be more open to us than those who know us. And besides, the people outside of our church groups are the ones who really need to hear God's messages. Otherwise, they will be lost.

....

25 · **Elisha Leads an Army**

2 KINGS 6:8-23

W ho was a greater spy than James
Bond and a more successful
warrior than Rambo even though
he was neither spy nor warrior?

If you guessed Elisha, you're right. But how can some bald
prophet be a better spy than 007? He didn't even have a special gadget pen! And how could he be a better soldier than
Rambo? He never even blew up one attack helicopter! All
that stuff was unnecessary because Elisha had something
those other guys didn't: God. With God on his side, Elisha
didn't need any sophisticated bugging devices to listen in
on Israel's enemies, and he didn't need any rocket launch-
ers to defeat an army. If you don't believe it, just read on.

Israel was at war with its northern neighbor, Syria. When
the Syrian king said to his officers, "Let's get our troops moving over here," Elisha also knew about it. He went to Israel's
king and said, "Hey, King, whatever you do, don't go over
here, because Syria's army is going to be there." The king
checked it out, and sure enough, Elisha was right. He saved
the king and his army. And this was not a fluke—Elisha did
this many times over.

After a few times of this, the Syrian king got frustrated. He
called his officers together and asked, "OK, who's the guy
who's selling us out? Who's spying for Israel?"

"Don't look at us!" the Syrian officers answered. "It's Elisha, the prophet! This guy tells Israel's king everything you
say, even what you say in your bedroom!"

....

The point here is not that God's going to tell you when some bullies are going to try to stuff you in a locker, or whether or not that special someone in math will go to the dance with you if you ask. The point is rather that no one can have any secrets from God. The Syrians were trying to win a battle, but God was aware of their plans; he even knew what the Syrian king was singing in the shower! When other people oppose us or Christian values, 2 Kings 6 can help us remember that nothing they do is a surprise to God. And if God knows what's happening, he is also able to plan and help us no matter what happens.

....

The king of Syria learned that Elisha was at the Israelite city of Dothan, so he ordered his men, "Send an army there to capture him!"

So the next morning, Elisha and his servant woke up to see the Syrian army camped at the gates of the city. Elisha's servant freaked. All he saw was a huge army against two men. But Elisha told the man, "Our army is bigger than theirs!" Then, praying to God, Elisha said, "Lord, open his eyes and let him see!" The next moment the servant *did* see the army Elisha meant— there were fiery horses and chariots all over the

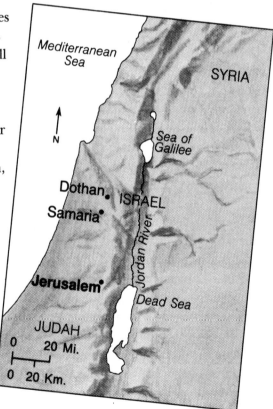

mountaintop! Next, Elisha prayed that the enemy be blinded—and they were.

And then, in what has to be the Old Testament equivalent of the hey-your-shoe's-untied gag, Elisha went out to the soldiers and said, "Hey, fellas, you're at the wrong city. Follow me; I'll take you to the guy you're looking for." And they bought it! The whole army! So Elisha led an entire army straight into Samaria, Israel's capital city. Let's see Rambo try that!

Now that the Syrian army was finally where they ultimately wanted to be if they were to control Israel, they were in a bind, totally at the mercy of their enemy. Israel's king wanted to kill them all, but Elisha talked him into feeding them all before letting them go home. Once they returned to Syria, there was peace between the two nations for a while.

....

Much can be learned about a person by how he treats his enemy. Israel could have killed the enemy army, but that would have been cold-blooded murder. Instead, Elisha wanted the soldiers to not only see (or, rather, to be blinded by) the power of God but also to have them see God's compassion by letting them go. Many Syrians, like Naaman (see 2 Kings 5), may have come to believe and trust in God after this event. How do we treat our enemies, especially if they are at our mercy? Do we pay them back for the pain they've caused us (by shoving us into a locker, for instance)? Or do we treat them as we want to be treated? That is the Golden Rule, to treat others as we wish to be treated (see Matt. 7:12). It won't be as much fun at first as revenge, but it will make us feel better about ourselves and let other people see Jesus in us.

....

26 · Jonah's Roundabout Journey

God's prophets were generally obedient people, right? Isaiah, Jeremiah, and Nathan, for example, were all faithful to God's commands. Oh, sure, there were the false prophets, but they don't count since they didn't commit themselves to following God in the first place. Well, one of God's most famous prophets is best known for his disobedience . . . and the consequences of his actions.

Jonah was this unwilling prophet's name, and the job he tried to refuse was a missionary journey to Nineveh, a very important city of Assyria, which happened to be Israel's enemy. In all fairness to Jonah, Assyria was a pretty nasty empire, even as empires go. They really didn't deserve to hear God's message. And God wouldn't be too put out if Jonah declined this mission and accepted an assignment that was safer and more pleasant. Right? Wrong! God had other plans for Jonah and Nineveh.

"Go to the great city of Nineveh, and give them this announcement from the Lord: 'I am going to destroy you, for your wickedness rises before me,'" God said to Jonah.

We don't know how Jonah answered God when he got this message, but we do know what he did. He promptly headed southwest to the coastal city of Joppa and got on a westbound boat bound for Tarshish (which was possibly Spain). The problem was that (1) Nineveh was about a five-hundred-mile trek *northeast* of Israel (in modern-day

Iran), and (2) you didn't need a boat to get there since the trip was across a desert.

Since God created the world, he definitely knew the difference between west and northeast. Needless to say, Jonah had not succeeded in fooling God about his plans. Once Jonah's ship was out on the Mediterranean, God struck up a great storm that threatened to break the ship apart. The sailors panicked, and after finding out Jonah was running from God and was responsible for their situation, they reluctantly tossed Jonah overboard to appease God and save their ship.

....

God knows everything, so you can't fool him. Don't even bother trying.

....

But God wasn't going to let Jonah die; Jonah wasn't going to get out of preaching to Nineveh that easily. Soon after Jonah hit the waves, God arranged for a great fish to come and swallow him, and for three days and nights Jonah sat inside a fish.

On the third day, Jonah called out to God: "I sank beneath the waves, and death was very near. The waters closed above me; the seaweed wrapped itself around my head. . . . When I had lost all hope,

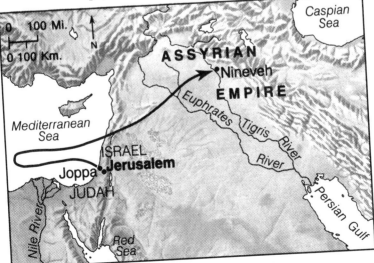

I turned my thoughts once more to the Lord. . . . I will never worship anyone but you! For how can I thank you enough for all you have done? I will surely fulfill my promises." Those were the words and the attitude God had wanted from Jonah. He ordered the fish to swim to shore and spit Jonah up.

Now God commanded Jonah again to preach to Nineveh, and this time Jonah headed off in the right direction. He came to the great city and spoke God's message to the people. And, believe it or not, they repented and worshiped the Lord.

....

Jonah thought that the people of Nineveh were too evil to deserve God's message; and even if they did hear it, they certainly would be too evil to turn from their ways and follow God. Jonah was wrong—no one is too evil to hear God's message of salvation, and no one is too evil to become a Christian. If you feel God calling you to share your faith with the school bully or some of the "stoners," don't try to run away from God. Ask him to give you the strength and the opportunity to do what he asks of you. After all, what if someone had considered you too evil to deserve God's forgiveness?

....

27 · **Israel Taken Captive**

Did you ever know anyone who had to give a bully lunch money so he wouldn't get beaten up? If so, then you have a pretty good handle on Israel's relationship with the Assyrian Empire. Basically, Israel's kings had to pay the Assyrian kings money or Israel would get beaten up.

This kind of activity went on all the time. Rather than spending a ton of money on a war, a strong kingdom or empire would simply say to some smaller country, "Hey, I could take you over, but I'm feeling generous. If you promise to pay me this much money, I'll let you maintain your freedom. If not, I'll send my army in and take over the whole country." As you can see, it was an offer the smaller country couldn't refuse. In its heyday, even Israel accepted tribute (that's what the money paid to a powerful kingdom was called) from neighboring lands.

But why didn't God protect Israel from Assyria? The Assyrians would have been no match for God, right? Right. But Israel never asked God for his help. The kings of Israel were idol-worshiping, evil men who ignored God and his teachings. It was for this very reason that God sent Assyria to attack Israel, as punishment for Israel's sin. All Israel needed to do was to confess their sins and ask God for help, and he would have spared them, just as he had spared the Assyrian capital of Nineveh fifty years before this event (see the book of Jonah). Instead of repenting, Israel bought off its enemies, time and time again.

....

The rules for people haven't changed much over the past few thousand years. Sin is still offensive to God, and he still wants us to follow him. God still punishes sin and still saves those who confess their sins to him. The major difference between then and now is that we can have eternal safety from our enemies. When we ask Jesus to save us from sin, we are saved forever. We don't have to keep paying him to continue to be saved. It was a once-and-for-all deal. We can ask Jesus for his help, and we can trust in him to rescue us. And even if he doesn't physically save us from a particular dilemma, we are eternally saved.

....

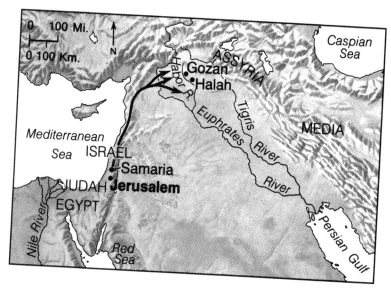

No more. King Hoshea, after paying tribute for several years, refused to pay any more. He made an agreement, not with God but with King So of Egypt to join forces and free Israel from its oppression. But this plan was discovered, and King Shalmaneser brought an army to Samaria to crush Hoshea. At the end of a three-year siege, in 722 B.C., the northern kingdom of Israel existed no more.

   The Assyrians had a wonderful policy of removing conquered people from their native land and then resettling that
land with people loyal to Assyria. This way no one would
revolt in the outer reaches of the empire, and all would be
peaceful. King Sargon (who ruled after Shalmaneser died)
deported the Israelites and sent them to live in colonies by
the Habor River, which fed into the northern part of the
Euphrates River, and into the land of the Medes, which is
now called Iran. Assyrians resettled the land of Israel and
intermarried with the few Israelites left. They came to be
known as Samaritans, the same people who would be hated
by the Jews in Jesus' day.

28 · God Fights for Judah

2 KINGS 18–19; 2 CHRONICLES 32

Thisis a day of trouble, insult, and dishonor. . . . Yet perhaps the Lord your God has heard the Assyrian general defying the living God and will rebuke him. Oh, pray for the few of us who are left."

This was the message King Hezekiah sent to Isaiah after Sennacherib attacked Judah. The problem started when King Hezekiah refused to pay tribute to Assyria any longer, thinking Judah could stand alone. Sennacherib attacked quickly as he headed west and south to discipline his unruly western border. He smashed Judah's fortified cities on his way to Jerusalem. Hezekiah gave him $1.5 million to go away and leave them alone; he took the money, but continued the attack. From Libnah, he issued an ultimatum to Judah, saying that they couldn't stand against his army. No other nation's gods had been able to protect them, so he figured Judah's God wouldn't be able to, either—especially since Hezekiah had broken down the altars in the hills. When Hezekiah had heard the threats, he ripped his clothes (a sign of grief), put on sackcloth, and sent this message to Isaiah.

Isaiah's reply was, "The Lord says, 'Tell your master not to be troubled by the sneers these Assyrians have made against me.' For the king of Assyria will receive bad news from home and will decide to return; and the Lord will see to it that he is killed when he arrives there."

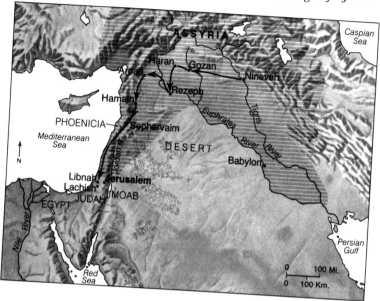

....

Why did God choose to save Judah this time? He let Israel be captured and had allowed Judah to be defeated many times. Why rescue them now? The main reason was that Hezekiah was a good king. He turned from his father's evil ways, repaired the Temple, began regular worship activities again, tore down idols and altars in the hills, and obeyed all of Moses' commands. Judah was finally doing right, so God protected them, or they allowed God to protect them. When we rebel against God, we shut him out of our life. Since God doesn't force himself on any of us, he cannot work to help us if we won't listen to him or even admit he's there. When we face a hopeless situation (like Hezekiah did), God can help us only if we are open to his suggestions and are looking for his help.

....

Sennacherib got word that the king of Ethiopia was about to attack him. So, before heading south to meet the attack, he left one final message for Judah: "Don't be fooled by that god you trust in. Don't believe it when he says that I won't conquer Jerusalem. . . . Have the gods of the other nations delivered them . . . ? The former kings of Assyria destroyed them all!"

Spreading this letter from Sennacherib out before God in the Temple, Hezekiah cried out, "Listen to this man's defiance of the living God. Lord, it is true that the kings of Assyria have destroyed all those nations and have burned their idol-gods. But they weren't gods at all; they were destroyed because they were only things that men had made of wood and stone. O Lord our God, we plead with you to save us from his power; then all the kingdoms of the earth will know that you alone are God."

And again, through Isaiah, God answered the king's prayer. "My command concerning the king of Assyria is that he shall not enter this city. . . . He shall return by the road he came, for I will defend and save this city for the sake of my own name and for the sake of my servant David."

That night the angel of God entered the Assyrian camp and killed 185,000 men. Sennacherib then returned to Nineveh, probably to raise another army. But he never made it back, for his sons killed him while he was praying to his god. Jerusalem was safe for as long as the people obeyed God.

....

Bad people will be judged by God sooner or later. Sennacherib had been evil for a long time, and he looked like he was getting away with it. But when he attacked Jerusalem, he was way too arrogant to be allowed victory. He insulted God, and God would not let him get away with such blasphemy. His time for justice had come. Ironically, he was killed while at the temple of the god who was supposed to have been protecting him. As demonstrated in this episode, we have little to fear from God's enemies. God can control them and bring about miraculous solutions to our problems. God is still at work today, even though we might not see many miracles or hear any messages from prophets. We can still depend on him to aid us in times of trouble. Let's not ever forget that!

....

29 · The Battle of Carchemish

2 CHRONICLES 35:20; JEREMIAH 46:2

There are some battles that stand out as significant events in history: Waterloo, where Napoleon was defeated by the English; the Battle of the Bulge, Hitler's last attempt to fend off the Allies; and, in ancient times, the battle of Jericho, which marked the beginning of the Israelite conquest of the Promised Land. Another of history's hallmark battles was the battle at Carchemish.

The Middle Eastern world was in turmoil. Assyria, the dominant force in the region for the past three hundred years, was crumbling. While it had for many years controlled Egypt and Israel, it had now lost control of these areas. In 612 B.C. Babylon captured its capital, Nineveh (in present-day northern Iraq). Babylon had basically conquered the Assyrian Empire at this time, but Assyria's king tried ruling from another city, Harran, only to be defeated again three years later.

....

You may be asking, "Hey! What does any of this have to do with the Bible? This isn't going to help me get along in life. Why do I have to know a bunch of battle stuff?" While this subject may not be normally taught in Sunday school, it is, nevertheless, important to know. This sets biblical events in context so that you can appreciate the history behind what happened. God spoke to Israel through Habakkuk, "Look, and be amazed! You will be astounded at what I am about to do! For I am going to do something in your lifetime that you will have to see to believe. I am raising a new force on the world scene, the Chaldeans, a cruel and violent nation who will march across the world and conquer it" (Hab. 1:5-6). In a few short years, Babylon accomplished what God predicted and controlled the known world. God's prophets spoke not only about repenting and following God; they also foretold political and military events. There's nothing God doesn't know!

....

It was at this point that Judah entered the story. Pharaoh Neco of Egypt, an ally of Assyria, couldn't stand by and watch his friends be destroyed—and he thought Egypt had a chance to become the dominant power again. So he marched his troops to Harran to help the Assyrians retake the city. On his way there, though, he had to pass through Judah. King Josiah, choosing the Babylonians over the Egyptians, attacked Neco's army at Megiddo. This proved unfortunate for Josiah, as he was killed in battle. Neco replaced Josiah's successor with Eliakim, charged Judah tribute money, and then continued on his way to Harran, which lay between Nineveh and Carchemish. Neco and the Assyrians failed to recapture the city, but Neco was able to gain control of much of the territory west of there.

In 605 B.C. the clock struck high noon—

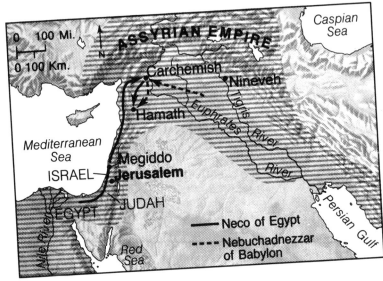

Babylon called out Egypt for a shootout. King Nebuchadnez-zar (made famous in the book of Daniel) marched his army into the city of Carchemish, crushing the Egyptian army very quickly. They ran away to Hamath in Syria, but Nebu-chadnezzar chased them and destroyed their army. With Assyria annihilated and Egypt so soundly defeated, Babylon controlled all the land west of them, as well as the rest of the Middle East—all the way to the Persian Gulf.

30 · Judah Exiled

2 KINGS 24–25; 2 CHRONICLES 36

Now that Babylon controlled most of the Middle East, Nebuchadnezzar thought, *I've got to make sure I control that major trade route* [that connected Africa, the Middle East, and Asia], *or doing business with the rest of the world is going to be rather difficult. And I better make sure Egypt doesn't try anything, either.* Unfortunately for Judah, they were between Babylon's army and Egypt, and their land lay along that important trade route. This, coupled with the fact that Judah's king was appointed by the Egyptian pharaoh Neco, meant that Judah was between Iraq and a hard place.

Nebuchadnezzar's first visit to Jerusalem was to collect the tribute promised him by Jehoiakim (also called Eliakim) while on his way to battle Egypt. It was at this visit, or invasion, that Nebuchadnezzar took many of the royalty, the skilled workers, and the talented young people and brought them to Babylon to be trained and made a part of Babylonian society. This gave the empire a source of new talent and kept Judah in a state of dependence. Since the ambitious, skilled men were taken away, no one was really able to lead and sustain a revolt. But Jehoiakim tried, probably after Babylon suffered a defeat in its war with Egypt in 601 B.C.

Babylon's setback didn't last long, and its rebuilt army marched to Jerusalem in 598 B.C. and laid siege to the city, capturing it in the spring of 597. Once again, Nebuchadnezzar took away the most promising Jews. He also brought

Jehoiakim to Babylon and set up a new king, Jehoiachin, in his place. He didn't last long—only three months—before he was exiled by Nebuchadnezzar, who put yet another king, Zedekiah, over Judah.

Zedekiah, too, forgot how powerful Babylon was, and he rebelled against Nebuchadnezzar. The Babylonian army came to lay siege to Jerusalem, intending to

destroy it. God told the people through the prophet Jeremiah, "Take your choice of life or death! Stay here in Jerusalem and die—slaughtered by your enemies, killed by starvation and disease— or go out and surrender to the Chaldean army and live. For I have set my face against this city" (Jer. 21:8-10). The people stubbornly ignored God, who allowed Nebuchadnezzar to conquer and burn down Jerusalem in 587 B.C. The walls were torn down, the buildings demolished, and the Temple, the pride of Israel, was looted and destroyed. Judah existed no more, and the rest of the inhabitants were carried off to Babylon.

91

....

How could God allow such a thing to happen to his people? Why didn't he save them from Babylon? The answer is easy:

God had run out of patience with Judah. It saw Israel destroyed for its evil ways 120 years before and did not learn its lesson. The prophets spoke to them, warning of the disasters to come if the nation did not repent, but Judah didn't listen. Then God said, "If you won't pay attention to my words, maybe some action will make you perk up." So he sent Nebuchadnezzar to destroy the nation. It did work: The Jews haven't worshiped another idol or false god from the Exile to the present. Let's hope God doesn't need to do anything so drastic to get us to pay attention to his words of correction when we are goofing up. The examples of Israel, Judah, and other nations and individuals in the Bible are there so we can learn from their mistakes and see the consequences of wrong actions. Each time we read a story like this, we should ask ourselves, What can I learn from this? Am I doing anything this person (or people) is doing? What can I do so I don't wind up in the same trouble they did? The answers are in the Bible, too. We can look at the Prophets, the Gospels, and the Epistles to learn what God wants us to do.

31 · The Medo-Persian Empire
DANIEL 7:1–8:10

Throughout the Bible many empires are mentioned. Some, like the Roman Empire, are quite famous for their many accomplishments. Others are known primarily for what happened in the Bible. The Medo-Persian Empire is one of these empires. Of course, its people may have accomplished some wonderful things in their time, but most people know them as the people who released the Jews from captivity. Or as the guys who threw Daniel to the lions. Or as the nation that, through Haman's plan, tried to exterminate the Jews, only to be foiled by Esther and Mordecai.

But where was the Medo-Persian Empire located? How did it get to be so powerful? Did anyone know they would ever come to power? I'm glad you asked.

The Medo-Persian Empire was a confederation of two nations, Media and Persia. The Medes were from northwest Iran, up by the Caspian Sea. The Persians were from Persia, east of the Caspian Sea and south all the way to the Persian Gulf (even extending east of this map). The Medes created a lot of problems for the Assyrian Empire and were responsible for the fall of Nineveh in 612 B.C. (Remember what Jonah prophesied to Nineveh about a hundred years earlier?) However, Babylonia became the dominant power soon after the fall of Nineveh, and the Medes would have to wait. The Persians, on the other hand, weren't strong enough to stand up to Assyria, but they were able to defeat the Medes in 550 B.C.

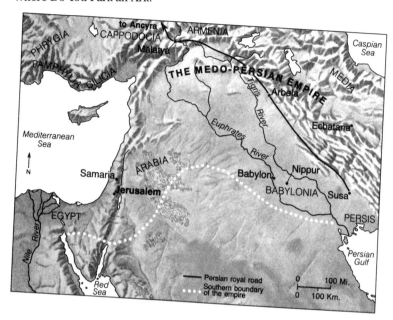

Cyrus of Persia then added the title "King of the Medes" to his name and thus united the two kingdoms. Eleven years later Cyrus's armies marched into Babylon, overtaking the city and its empire. Medo-Persia remained the dominant empire until 331 B.C., when Alexander the Great of Greece conquered it.

At its height, the Medo-Persian Empire possessed lands in India, southern Russia, most of the Middle East, Egypt, Asia Minor, and the lands of Thrace, east of Greece. Its way of governing these vast areas was to appoint local people as governors and administrators, thus giving the conquered enough freedom to be happy, but not enough to be dangerous. That explains why people like Daniel, Ezra, and Nehemiah could be leaders in Persia and Judah.

And it may be of interest to note that God knew all of this would happen. Daniel's visions showed that Persia would become a world power (see Daniel's vision of the beasts in Dan. 7 and his vision of the ram in Dan. 8:2-4). The writing on the wall that Daniel interpreted for Belshazzar said that

Babylon would fall to the Persians. Isaiah even prophesied that a king named Cyrus would let the Jews rebuild Jerusalem and the Temple: "When I say of Cyrus, 'He is my shepherd,' he will certainly do as I say; and Jerusalem will be rebuilt and the Temple restored, for I have spoken it" (Isa. 44:28).

....

When Paul wrote in Romans 13:1, "Obey the government, for God is the one who has put it there. There is no government anywhere that God has not placed in power," he wasn't kidding. God is responsible for putting each empire in the past into power and each government today into power. And each one has its own place in God's work. Babylon punished Judah for its unfaithfulness, and Medo-Persia punished Babylon for its cruelty and sent the Jews back home. Even nations today are under God's authority, whether they want to admit it or not. It is important for us to obey our government, even if we don't believe that everything it does is right. Ultimately, God will determine how faithful our country has been; that is not our job. Instead, we should try to be the best citizens we can be.

....

32 · **The Journey Home to Jerusalem**

EZRA 1:1–3:6

T*he faithful Jews in Persia were restless.*

"Surely the Lord will remember us. We will be going home soon!

He promised us. Jeremiah wrote, 'You will be in Babylon for seventy years. But then I will come and do for you all the good things I have promised and bring you home again'" (Jer. 29:10).

"Yes," another agreed, "and remember what Isaiah wrote, 'When I say of Cyrus, "He is my shepherd," he will certainly do as I say; and Jerusalem will be rebuilt and the Temple restored'" (Isa. 44:28).

But many of the younger exiles who had never seen Jerusalem or the Temple didn't understand all the excitement. *We are home already,* they thought.

An old, bent man stood, leaning on a walking stick, and proclaimed to all who could hear, "I have been here about seventy years, since Nebuchadnezzar came and took the first of us away. Daniel and I came together. And now Babylon is crushed, and Cyrus is king. I am too old myself to make the journey back, but I will see the day you young people return to the Holy City."

That day did come. In 538 B.C., King Cyrus proclaimed to the amazed Jews, "Cyrus, king of Persia, hereby announces that Jehovah, the God of heaven who gave me my vast empire, has now given me the responsibility of building him a Temple in Jerusalem, in the land of Judah. All Jews throughout the kingdom may now return to Jerusalem to rebuild this Temple of Jehovah, who is the God of Israel and of Jerusalem. May his blessings rest upon you" (Ezra 1:2-3). Cyrus even gave back to the Jews the items that Nebuchadnezzar had stolen from the Temple many years before.

....

Can you imagine the excitement this must have caused? Living to see the words of the prophets fulfilled? These Jews in Persia must have been extremely moved by God's working in their lives, by seeing actual evidence of God's presence! If only God would do things like that for us, right? Well, his promises do come true, but we just have to wait. These Jews only had seventy years to wait for God; we have no idea when he will fulfill the last of his promises—the return of Jesus. It could be another two thousand years, or it could be while we're watching reruns of "Gilligan's Island" next week. No matter when God chooses to send Jesus back, we should be expecting his return, energized by the truth that it will happen.

....

The leaders, priests, and Levites were certainly anxious to return, so they immediately began planning and collecting their supplies. Those who chose to remain in Persia and not make the eight-hundred-mile trip contributed gifts and assistance to the brave,

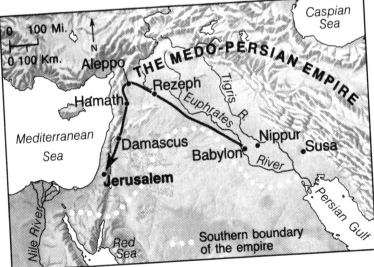

adventurous Jews who were to make a trip of a lifetime. So everyone played a part in bringing about God's plans.

In all, forty-three thousand Jews left the safe, comfortable surroundings of Persia and began the long journey back to the Holy Land—a journey that took at least four months of marching, camping, marching, camping, and more marching. They followed the Euphrates River northeast, ensuring plenty of water and food for the large group. Then, after reaching Aleppo in Syria, they headed south for home. But once they reached Judah, they were greeted by the ruins of cities and towns that had been destroyed for seventy years. The work was just beginning.

In September, all the people gathered in Jerusalem for a party. This was the time of year that the Feast of Tabernacles was celebrated, and the people were very willing to thank God for their safe trip and to ask for his continued care for them. Zerubbabel, one of the Jewish leaders, and the priests rebuilt the altar and offered sacrifices. This feast must have had special meaning for these Jews, for God had intended the Feast of Tabernacles to be celebrated so his people would remember their exodus from Egypt and how they had to live in tents and trust in God. After their long journey, they probably really understood the meaning of the feast.

....

God will often time things so perfectly in our lives that we can easily see his hand. For example, we make a commitment at Christmas or Easter to follow Christ, and the celebration of that holiday takes on new meaning or reinforces our decision. That's what God did for these Jews: He timed their arrival so that their first feast, the Feast of Tabernacles, took on a special meaning for them and they were better able to understand what it must have been like on the first occasion of the feast a thousand years before.

....

The Temple construction wouldn't begin until the next June, but the people of God had taken the first big step in reestablishing God's nation, the nation Christ would come from to save the earth!

33 · The Rebuilding of Jerusalem's Walls

NEHEMIAH 2:11–4:23; 6:1-19

The year was 445 B.C., and the city of Jerusalem was a disgrace. About ninety years before, the first wave of exiles, led by Zerubbabel, returned from Persia to resettle their homeland and rebuild the Lord's Temple. But after all that time the city walls and gates were still in ruins. Nehemiah, a devout Jew and cup-bearer for the Persian king Artaxerxes, heard about the situation in Jerusalem and wept and cried out to God, hoping God would hear him and allow him to go to Jerusalem and rebuild the walls. God listened and arranged for Nehemiah to make the long, difficult journey back to the land of his fathers, taking basically the same (though actually a little shorter) path that Zerubbabel and the first wave of exiles took ninety-two years earlier.

....

It's hard for us today to understand why walls were so important to a city. Now that we have airplanes, helicopters, rockets, and missiles, walls would provide us with no protection at all. But in ancient times, up through the early 1800s, walls were important defenses that kept invaders out of castles and cities. If an army wanted to attack a city, it would have to either scale the walls, break down a wall and march in, or lay siege to the city and hope to starve the people out. Once the walls were breached, the city was doomed. Times have changed, but the need to be safe has not, and Jerusalem was definitely not safe as long as the walls were piles of rubble.

....

A few days after arriving, Nehemiah secretly toured the city's boundaries to check on how bad the walls were. Then he went to the people of the city and said, "You know full well the tragedy of our city; it lies in ruins and its gates are burned. Let us rebuild the wall of Jerusalem and rid ourselves of this disgrace!"

And when the people heard that the king approved the project, they answered, "Good! Let's rebuild the wall!"

So Nehemiah and the people of Jerusalem began. Nehemiah divided up the labor so each group of people had one small section of the wall to work on. In all, forty-one groups worked on forty-one sections of the wall, with many people working on sections of the wall that were near their homes. Talk about an incentive to put in quality work! Nobody would want his home and treasure to be in the path of an angry army, unless he wanted to see what it felt like to be caught in a stampede!

As the Jews worked, enemies taunted and teased them, saying, "If even a fox walked along the top of their wall, it would collapse!" But Nehemiah kept praying to God and encouraging his people, and soon they had rebuilt the wall to half its original height. And when Sanballat, Tobiah, Geshem, and

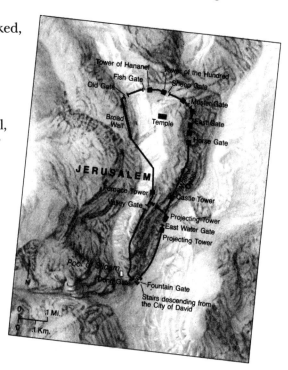

Israel's other enemies saw that the work was going well, they increased the pressure on the Jews, trying to make them stay away from the city and plotting attacks. At this point, people had to split shifts in order to defend themselves, with half of the people building and the other half watching for enemies.

Nehemiah was even in danger of losing his life. Five times, his enemies sent messages asking him to meet them outside the city, where they intended to kill him. But Nehemiah saw through their weak attempt and refused to leave. They even tried to discredit Nehemiah, hoping to scare him into entering the Temple, thus disobeying God's laws. Nothing stopped Nehemiah and the people of Jerusalem from finishing their job, and finishing in record time. The whole project took only fifty-two days. The city was safe, and Jerusalem was again ready to be the city of God.

....

If anything's worth doing, it's worth doing right. And if anything's worth doing, there are going to be plenty of people to stop you from doing it. Like Nehemiah, we may find us taking on a project that looks way too huge to accomplish, but is very important to us or to God. The way to do it is to divide up the big job into many little jobs, and before you know it, the big job is done. And don't forget the most important part of any job—prayer! If God asks you to do something for him, he'll be there to help and encourage.

....

34 · Joseph and Mary Take a Road Trip

MATTHEW 2:1-8; LUKE 2:1-7

J oseph, it's been almost nine months
since . . ." The young
woman's voice trailed off as she
looked down at her stomach.

Then, with a hopeful gaze, she asked, "Do we have to go
to Bethlehem?"

Joseph breathed a heavy sigh. "Yes, Mary, we do. There
really isn't a choice in the matter. We'll finish packing up
tonight, and then we'll be on the road early tomorrow
morning." He noticed his wife's put-out expression. "The
sooner we get there, the sooner we can get back. Do you
want to have the baby on the road?"

Mary shrugged her shoulders and reluctantly went off to
finish preparing for the trip to Bethlehem. *Why couldn't
Augustus have waited a few more weeks to declare this census,* Mary
wondered. *Doesn't he know how hard these long journeys are on
pregnant women?*

Of course she knew Caesar hadn't done this to inconve-
nience her. The order for the census had probably been
signed many months ago, and by the time the order came
from Rome by ship to Caesarea (the Roman capital city in
the province of Judea), then from Caesarea to the many
towns and cities in Judea, Mary was about due.

Mary didn't realize at the time just how God was arranging
things. Yes, she was about to give birth, and it wouldn't be a

pleasant trip to Bethlehem. But the Messiah was to be born in Bethlehem (see Mic. 5:2), and if God wanted to use an emperor's census to get the parents to the right town at the right time, there was no reason why he couldn't. Many times God will work in ways that we don't expect, even using non-Christians to accomplish his tasks. We should constantly be watching for God's hand in our lives, because if we're not careful, we could miss it while we're looking another way.

....

"Tell me again why we have to go to Bethlehem," Mary asked Joseph as they made their way south from the Galilean village of Nazareth.

Joseph put down his pack and motioned for Mary to sit down on a large rock by the side of the road. "You see, Rome has decided to make us part of the Roman Empire. And since they did that, we have to pay taxes to Rome. So Caesar commanded that a census be taken so he knows how much tax money he should collect from us."

"But why Bethlehem?" Mary asked.

"Because that's where my family is from. It's all part of the deal when you're from the line of David." Joseph smiled at Mary. "It's all part of the bureaucracy. Our coming to my home village makes their bookkeeping easier."

As they sat

103

discussing the politics of the empire, another group of travelers had passed them on their way to Jerusalem, Bethel, or even Bethlehem. Joseph and Mary watched as they went by.

Joseph helped Mary up and said, "That's the tenth group to pass us so far, but we're just about to Jericho. We've only got about another twenty miles to go." Slowly they continued on.

An hour later, after yet another group passed them, Mary became worried. "Joseph! What if we can't find a place to stay? I've slowed us up so. Where will we sleep?"

Holding his wife's hand, Joseph reassured her. "Don't worry about our pace. You can't expect to keep up with the others. We'll be fine. Even if it means we have to sleep in a stable, we'll be fine. God has special plans for this child," Joseph said as he patted Mary's stomach, "and he won't let something happen to us now."

35 · **Jesus Begins His Ministry**

JOHN 1:29–2:13

Look! *There is the Lamb of God who takes away the world's sin! He was the one I was talking about when I said, 'Soon a man far greater than* I am is coming, who existed long before me!' " John the Baptist eagerly pointed out Jesus to those around him as he saw Jesus. John had baptized Jesus at least a month and a half earlier, possibly at this spot east of the Jordan River (right about where the *R* in *River* is on the map), and now he told of the events of that baptism, especially of the Holy Spirit descending upon Jesus.

The next day, too, Jesus came walking toward John. The Baptist said to two of his own disciples, "See! There is the Lamb of God!" With those words, John the Baptist pointed these two men to the Source of eternal life, and they became Jesus' first disciples. Those men were Andrew and John.

Andrew was so excited about finding Jesus that he went looking for his brother, Simon. He told Simon the news and brought him to Jesus. It was then that Jesus said to Andrew's brother, "You are Simon, John's son—but you shall be called Peter, the rock!"

The next day Jesus left this wilderness by the Jordan and headed for Galilee, possibly taking the Jericho Road north to his hometown of Nazareth. While in Galilee Jesus met Philip, who, in turn, told his friend Nathanael about Jesus. "Nazareth! Can anything good come from there?" he asked Philip scornfully. To the Jews of Jesus' day, Nazareth was a waste of space on a map. The small town was near major trade routes, and pious Jews did not appreciate that the Nazarenes dealt so frequently with the unclean Gentiles who used the road. Also, because Nazareth was surrounded by mountains on three sides and by the "unclean" trade routes, the city maintained a certain isolation from the rest of the area. These two facts led to Nathanael's rejection of anything positive coming from this town. When he did go and meet Jesus, he was soon convinced that at least one thing of worth came from Nazareth.

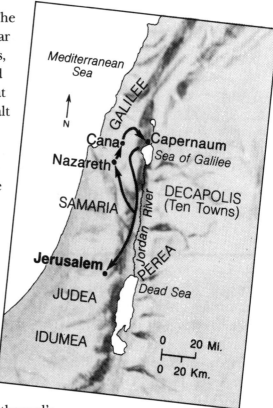

....

Telling people about Jesus can be a scary thing. It's easy to talk about him with people in church or youth group, but mentioning Jesus to friends and classmates can be social suicide. Who wants to hang around with a "Jesus freak," right? Andrew took a chance by telling Peter about Jesus, and Peter responded immediately. Don't we wish all our witnessing attempts went that easy? Nathanael wasn't such a pushover, though. His response was more like we'd expect to hear when we talk to others about Jesus. When Nathanael practically laughed in Philip's face, Philip didn't leave and never tell anyone about Jesus again. Nor did he attempt to overcome Nathanael's prejudice and argue with him. Instead, he simply said, "Just

come and see for yourself." Ultimately, that is what we all must do when we talk about Jesus—we must let others decide for themselves by seeing what Jesus is all about. God will do the actual converting, but we must do what we can—even if it means taking a risk.

....

Once Jesus reached Nazareth, Mary, Jesus' mother, invited Jesus and his disciples to a wedding a few miles north of there in the village of Cana. It was here that Jesus performed his first miracle—turning water into wine. The wedding celebration (which could have lasted as long as a week!) had been going well, up to a point. The guests must have been particularly thirsty, for the wine had run out. Now to run out of wine at a wedding was a tragedy, sort of like running out of potato chips during a Super Bowl party. When Jesus' mother asked him to do something about the problem, he told the servants to fill the ceremonial water jars with water and take them to the master of ceremonies. When this man tasted what was in the jars, he was amazed. "This is wonderful stuff!" he told the groom. "You're different from most. Usually a host uses the best wine first, and afterwards, when everyone is full and doesn't care, then he brings out the less expensive brands. But you have kept the best for the last!" The servants must have been laughing their heads off at the puzzled groom and master of ceremonies.

After this, Jesus went to Capernaum for a few days and then headed to Jerusalem for the Passover.

....

Taking the old pots used for stale Jewish religious habits, Jesus turned the water there into fresh, high-quality wine. Rituals are important for they help us to focus on Jesus. But when rituals take the place of God (as they had for the Jews of Jesus' day), they become a problem. If we go to church and do churchy things and are bored by them, we may need to pause and look to Jesus, remembering why we do these things. We shouldn't drink the plain, lukewarm "water" of religion when we have excellent "wine" available in Jesus.

....

36 · Good News for Samaritans

JOHN 4

After Jesus' first visit to Jerusalem at the beginning of his ministry (when he spoke with Nicodemus), Jesus and his disciples went to the Jordan River, possibly near where John was baptizing, and baptized those who wanted to become his disciples. Meanwhile, the Pharisees learned that Jesus and his guys were baptizing more than John and his guys, and they intended to investigate. At this time, Jesus left Judea because the time was not right for a confrontation with the religious authorities. That would come later.

Leaving Judea, Jesus intended to go back to Galilee, where he based his ministry. But in order to do so, he and his disciples traveled through the territory of Samaria. Big, fat, hairy deal, right? To the Jews of Jesus' day, it was an incredibly big deal. A Jew entering Samaria was equivalent to a Nazi visiting a synagogue! The Jews' hatred for the Samaritans was so deep that they wouldn't even step foot on their soil unless they absolutely had to. To avoid such uncleanness, they would travel *around* Samaria to get where they wanted to go! This wasn't like just crossing the street to avoid meeting an ex-friend—we're talking walking around a whole territory. For instance, if a Jew wanted to go to Cana from Jerusalem, about a seventy-mile straight trip, he would cross the Jordan before entering Samaria, walk north in the Transjordan (the area east of the Jordan River), and then cross the river again when he was safely east of Galilee, making the journey at least 115 miles. In a car, that's about an extra hour; on foot, that's more like an extra day.

....

Is prejudice really worth it? It cost the Jews two days on any trip they made back and forth around Samaria. And Nathanael almost missed an opportunity to meet Jesus because of his prejudice against Nazarenes. Focusing on differences between races, sexes, nationalities, schools, etc. can only lead to separation. But they are minor in the grand scheme of things—we all breathe air, eat food, laugh and cry, live on the same planet, and are all children of God. To blindly hate another group because of superficial differences is a waste. We could be missing out on making a great friend or meeting an interesting person if we can't get past skin color, religion, or accents. Ultimately, it is we who lose by being prejudiced.

....

Once in Samaria, they stopped to rest at Jacob's Well, near the town of Sychar. (Jacob built this well after he settled in this area—see Gen. 33:17-20.) It was about noon, and a woman came to the well to get her water. They were alone, for Jesus' disciples had gone to get food, and everyone else got water in the morning or evening to avoid the heat. Then Jesus did something radical—he talked to the woman, asking her for a drink of water.

The woman was very surprised to have a Jewish man talk to her. In response to her surprise, Jesus said, "If you only knew what a wonderful gift God has for you, and who I am, you would ask me for some *living* water!"

"Where would you get this living water? And besides, are you greater than our ancestor Jacob? How can you offer better water than this which he and his sons and cattle enjoyed?" she asked, probably a little offended at an apparent slam against this national landmark.

He answered her, "The water I give them becomes a perpetual spring within them, watering them forever with eternal life."

Then after some discussion about the proper place to worship—whether in Jerusalem or on nearby Mount Gerizim, where Joshua pronounced blessings on the nation (see Josh. 8:33)—Jesus told her that soon it wouldn't matter *where* they worshiped, but *how* they worshiped—sincerely.

When she mentioned that the Christ would explain everything someday, Jesus told her straight out, "I am the Messiah!"

The woman headed back to Sychar to tell everyone there about Jesus. The townspeople came to him, inviting him and his disciples to stay, and many in that town believed in him.

....

The woman at the well began the day alone, avoided by the townspeople because of her immoral lifestyle. By the end of the day, she was responsible for leading many to believe in the Christ. Who knows, maybe a church even met in her home later. We are never too far gone for God to save us. No matter how bad we might have been or if we've only been Christians a short time, we, too, can tell people how they can be saved.

....

37 · **Amazing Events in Galilee**

MATTHEW 8:1-34

I f you were from Capernaum in New Testament times, you had a lot to brag about. You lived in a village on the shores of the Sea of Galilee, so you had a great fishing business. Your village had a Roman garrison (though many wouldn't have liked having Gentiles stationed there). And your village would have been Jesus' base of operations, with Jesus teaching many lessons and performing many miracles in and around your town. You didn't live in a city like Jerusalem, but Capernaum was important enough in the region to suit you.

And while others in the village did not particularly care a fig about Jesus and his miracles (see Matt. 11:23 for Jesus' later condemnation of your village), you did. In fact, you saw everything Jesus did when he was living in Capernaum.

You were a member of the large crowd gathered near a hill north of your village to listen to Jesus give his longest recorded sermon, the Sermon on the Mount. You stood and listened as Jesus sat on that hillside and gave the Beatitudes (Matt. 5:1-10) and the Golden Rule (Matt. 7:12). His words captivated you; no one had ever spoken with such authority before. Amazed, you followed the crowd down from the mount and back to Capernaum.

You were near the front of the crowd when a leper approached Jesus and asked, "Sir, if you want to, you can heal me." Then Jesus actually *touched* the leper and replied, "I want to." He was healed! Right there!

When Jesus and the crowd entered the village, you heard a centurion refuse Jesus' offer to come to his home to heal a servant boy. "Sir," the Roman captain humbly said, "I am not worthy to have you in my home; [and it isn't necessary for you to come]. If you will only stand here and say, 'Be healed,' my servant will get well!" When Jesus answered him, "Go on home. What you have believed has happened!" you had no doubts that it did.

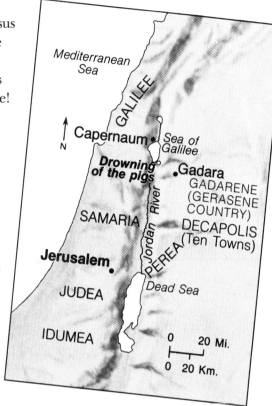

Later that night, you and your friends were talking about the day's unusual events—including how Jesus had healed the mother-in-law of Simon, now called Peter—when a storm struck over the sea. You all thought nothing of it, since storms always appeared suddenly. Because the Sea of Galilee was below sea level and surrounded by hills, the weather changed drastically there, with fierce winds and unpredictable storms commonplace. *The storm ended suddenly, more suddenly than it began,* you thought at the time. The next day it was rumored that when Jesus spoke from his boat on the sea, the storm stopped. Remarkable, but it did explain the abrupt end to the rain.

After Jesus' boat reached the southeastern shore of the sea, two demon-possessed men met him and his chosen disciples, and the men were afraid of Jesus. Then the demons inside of them pleaded, "What do you want with us, O Son of God? You have no right to torment us yet. If you cast us out, send us into that herd of pigs." When he did, the pigs stampeded over a cliff, falling into the sea. The people from the nearby town of Gadara complained for weeks about the loss to their incomes! But when you heard of this event, you praised God that the men were saved from their possession. You knew that you had indeed seen God.

....

As you read Matthew 8, did you imagine yourself there witnessing these events? Do you believe you would have reacted like this day's reading suggests? If you think you would have believed, do you also believe when miraculous things happen today? Even though Jesus doesn't walk among us, the Holy Spirit is here, carrying on Jesus' work. Many today dismiss unexplainable events and healings as flukes, and some say there is a logical explanation for them, though they can't think of one. Let's not deny God's involvement when we see something happen that seems to have no explanation. There is an explanation—God is alive and still performing miracles!

....

38 · **More Miracles Than You Can Shake a Stick At**

MATTHEW 15:21-39; MARK 7:24–8:10

Jesus' ministry was well into its second year at this point. But the religious leaders were still having problems accepting him and his works as coming from God. In fact, Jesus had just left a bunch of Pharisees who came from Jerusalem to bother him some more—this time about washing his hands before eating. Jesus, in short order, made them look rather silly, pointing out that it didn't matter if someone's hands were clean as long as his heart was (see Matt. 15:1-20). Rather than making them too angry before the appointed time, Jesus and his disciples left Galilee for Phoenicia, along the Mediterranean coast.

We assume Jesus came to this region to get some rest from the crowds. What tips us off is that he did not seem willing to help a woman in Tyre who came to him for help. When she asked Jesus to remove a demon from her daughter, Jesus wouldn't answer her. Finally, he said, "I was sent to help the Jews—the lost sheep of Israel—not the Gentiles."

When she wouldn't give up, Jesus told her, "It doesn't seem right to take the bread from the children and throw it to the dogs." These words sound harsh, but they reflected the Jews' attitude toward Gentiles—they were as dogs (who were wild and dirty, not like our pets today).

Playing along with Jesus' choice of words, she replied, "Yes, it is! For even the puppies beneath the table are permitted to eat the crumbs that fall."

Jesus was moved by her persistence, faith, and wit. She believed that just the "crumbs" of Jesus' power would be enough to heal her daughter. We imagine Jesus smiling as he said, "Woman, your faith is large, and your request is granted."

....

Even though Jesus was "on vacation," he still took time out to help others. Jesus did this time and time again. To be a true servant, we must be willing to help others even when we are relaxing or trying to rest. Time for ourselves is important (and Jesus got away to be alone and rest on many occasions), but our pleasure must not take priority over our friends and family. If a friend calls with a problem and we are on the couch watching our favorite show, do we turn off the TV and talk to her, or do we tell her we'll call back after the program? We don't need to give up all our free time and counsel everyone we meet—we just need to be less selfish with our time. The rewards for ourselves and others will make the time well spent.

....

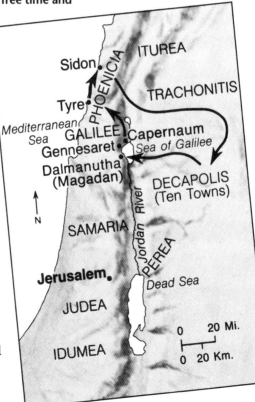

After his working vacation, Jesus returned to Galilee, but by way of the Ten Cities, an area east of the Sea of Galilee and the Jordan River.

This, too, was a Gentile area that was hellenized (followed Greek customs, not ruled by women named Helen) and out of the Jews' favor. This was an important trip for Jesus because it marked the fact that he had expanded his ministry to include Gentiles, not just Jews. What had changed since his conversation with the woman in Tyre and this moment is unknown to us, but the time had come for the Jews to see that Gentiles were to be a part of God's plan also.

Great crowds came to him in this region, and Jesus healed many people. While he was healing, Jesus must have also been teaching, for the people hung around for three days. At the end of this time, Jesus suggested to his disciples that they feed the crowds, who had no food left and were hungry. The disciples, even after having seen Jesus feed over five thousand men with a few loaves and fish, couldn't imagine how to feed the four-thousand-plus people here. Refreshing their memory, Jesus took the seven loaves and the few fish they had and, after giving thanks to God, distributed the food so everyone had plenty to eat.

....

There are no limits on who may come into God's kingdom. Anyone who believes that Jesus is God's Son and that he died to take away their sins is a Christian. Jesus had to demonstrate to his disciples and the other Jews—that Jews, Samaritans, and even Gentiles were eligible to be his followers. Since the majority of us are Gentiles, that is no longer a problem to understand. But we can still find ourselves saying that so-and-so is too mean, that this person drinks too much, or that that person sleeps around and is beyond saving. Such is not the case, though. This sort of prejudice is no different from hating people of a different color or nationality. Everyone is a potential Christian. Let's follow Jesus' example and offer the chance of salvation to anyone who wants it.

40 · Jesus' Last Week in Jerusalem

LUKE 19:28–21:38

Jesus' last week on earth was an eventful one. It began with Jesus and the disciples arriving at Bethphage and Bethany from Jericho. Jesus ordered his disciples to bring a donkey colt they would find in the next village. When they brought it back to Jesus, he mounted the animal and began his triumphal entry into Jerusalem. All along the two-mile ride from Bethany and over the Mount of Olives, people threw cloaks and palm leaves across his path and shouted, "Hosanna! God has given us a King! Long live the King! Let all heaven rejoice! Glory to God in the highest heavens!"

Some of the religious leaders in the crowd yelled at Jesus, "Rebuke your followers for saying things like that!" They thought the crowd was committing blasphemy by claiming Jesus as their King.

But Jesus answered them, "If they keep quiet, the stones along the road will burst into cheers!" Now that's a powerful image! As they neared Jerusalem, Jesus' mood changed from happiness to sadness, as he focused on Jerusalem's fate. Knowing what the next week held for him, Jesus cried, "Eternal peace was within your reach and you turned it down."

Entering the city through the East Gate, Jesus and his disciples came upon the Temple area. When Jesus saw the merchants and moneychangers there cheating the people, he repeated an act he performed when he began his ministry—he chased the merchants away and overturned their

39 · Jesus Raises Lazarus

JOHN 11:1-46

It was winter time, just after Hanukkah, and Jesus had left Jerusalem again after the religious leaders had tried to kill him. He went out to an area on the east side of the Jordan River, the place where John the Baptist had been baptizing. While there, many people who had seen and heard John the Baptist recognized that John's predictions about Jesus had come true, so they put their trust in Jesus.

His presence in this place must not have been a secret because Martha and Mary sent Jesus a message while he was in this area called Perea. Their message was, "Sir, your good friend is very, very sick"; the implied message was, "Jesus, please come here and heal our brother before he dies!" But Jesus, knowing the future, chose to remain where he was because he knew that God would receive glory from this situation.

Finally, after two days of waiting, Jesus announced they would go to Judea. The disciples couldn't believe it. "Only a few days ago the Jewish leaders in Judea were trying to kill you. Are you going there again?" they asked, hoping to talk Jesus out of doing such a self-destructive thing.

Jesus had to explain his motives: "Lazarus is dead. And for your sake, I am glad I wasn't there, for this will give you another opportunity to believe in me. Come, let's go to him."

Thomas, realizing that Jesus was determined and that

this could be the end of him and their three-year adventure, said, "Let's go too—and die with him." And so they went.

Where they were going was a potentially dangerous place. Bethany, Lazarus's hometown, was just two miles east of Jerusalem, located on the eastern side of the Mount of Olives. It was near enough that religious leaders had come to Beth-

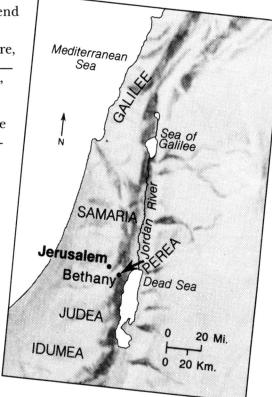

any for Lazarus's funeral and mourning period. With people there who wanted Jesus dead, the situation could have been explosive. It was also close enough to Jerusalem to ensure that word about this visit would spread fairly quickly, thus clueing the Jerusalem leaders in on his activities there.

When Jesus did arrive, he went to Lazarus's tomb and commanded him to come out. The mourners, especially the religious leaders, must have thought Jesus mad. But when Lazarus walked out of the tomb, many, including some of the religious leaders, changed their minds and believed in Jesus. Those who refused to believe that this was a sign of his deity went immediately to Jerusalem to tell on Jesus.

After this miracle, Jesus left Judea and went to G
a few months, until the time for his death had com

....

Why would Jesus choose to wait when he had an opp
to do good? First of all, Lazarus may have already bee
when the message got to Jesus. If Lazarus had been d
four days when Jesus arrived in Bethany, the two day:
waited before leaving and the day's travel to Bethany
to three days. Lazarus had probably been dead a day
Jesus received the message; thus, there was no reasor
Second, this event was important for Jesus' ministry. I
strated that Jesus had control over death and that he
Resurrection. Third, it also proved to be the straw tha
the Pharisees' backs. They could no longer dismiss Je:
was a threat to their power in Judea and had to be d
After this event, the Crucifixion would not be far off.
only see a part of the story when we ask Jesus for son
His delays in answering us may make it seem like he
care or that he can't do anything, but they may be n
for bringing about the larger plan. We should not on
Jesus to help us, we should also try to imagine oursel
big picture, how we fit into God's plans. It will help
patience if we can see beyond our own need and loo
those in God's kingdom.

....

tables. He shouted, "The Scriptures declare, 'My Temple is a place of prayer; but you have turned it into a den of thieves.'" Then, after things settled back down, Jesus sat down and began to teach the crowds in the Temple, demonstrating what the Temple was really for.

....

If Jesus was such a perfect guy, why did he get angry and trash the Temple? Wasn't that sinning? No, it wasn't. Jesus got angry because those people were dishonoring God by making money at a place of worship and for giving nonbelievers a wrong impression of God. What Jesus was demonstrating was something called righteous indignation, which is OK. We should be angry when people do things against God. To not care that someone is hurting God is just as bad as hurting him ourselves.

....

From this day, Sunday, through Thursday, Jesus sat and taught in the Temple, and each night he would return to Bethany to sleep. He taught people while answering the religious leaders' half-baked questions and accusations. Some of the subjects he covered were paying taxes, his authority, the afterlife, generosity, and sacrifice. Jesus even taught about the time of tribulation to come: False Messiahs will

Mediterranean Sea

GALILEE

Sea of Galilee

N

Jordan River

SAMARIA

PEREA

Jericho

Mount of Olives

Jerusalem

Bethphage

Bethany

Dead Sea

JUDEA

0   20 Mi.

0   20 Km.

IDUMEA

121

come; wars will break out; there will be earthquakes, famines, epidemics, and other horrifying things before the end of the age. Then after these signs have come and satanic forces have attacked Jerusalem, Jesus will return. He warned the people listening to him, perhaps hearing his voice for the last time, "Watch out! Don't let my sudden coming catch you unawares; don't let me find you living in careless ease, carousing and drinking, and occupied with the problems of this life, like all the rest of the world. Keep a constant watch."

....

With Jesus knowing his time was just about up, he gave these final words of warning to those who would listen to him. And now, almost two thousand years later, those words of warning still apply, maybe more so because the time of Jesus' return is even closer. As we watch the news and read in the paper, many wars, natural disasters, and epidemics occur all the time. Almost all of the prophecy in the Bible has been fulfilled. The time is near. We should be on the watch, trying to live like Christ wants us to because he could come back soon.

....

41 · **Another Snake in Another Garden**

MATTHEW 26:36-56; MARK 14:32-52; LUKE 22:39-53; JOHN 18:1-11

J esus and his followers had just finished the Last Supper, a celebration of the Passover Feast and a dinner initiating what we call Communion. Leading eleven of his chosen disciples, Jesus headed for the Garden of Gethsemane. This garden, located on the western slope of the Mount of Olives, was a place Jesus had come to many times before to be alone with his Father and pray. This night was to be the last time he would come here.

As they entered, Jesus led Peter, James, and John farther into the garden with him and told them, "My soul is crushed with horror and sadness to the point of death . . . stay here . . . stay awake with me." Then he went off by himself and prayed, "My Father! If it is possible, let this cup be taken away from me. But I want your will, not mine." Luke, a doctor, tells us that Jesus was so distressed that his sweat was like drops of blood.

Jesus prayed this prayer three times, and after each prayer he returned to the three disciples and found them asleep. On the third time back to them, Jesus said, "Up! Let's be going! Look! Here comes the man who is betraying me!" Jesus wanted them to get up so they could all go to where the other disciples were waiting so no one would get hurt and he could control the situation.

123

....

Doing what God asks of us can often be very difficult. Abraham, Moses, David, the prophets, and others faced many dangers working for God. Jesus faced death to do what needed to be done. And notice that Jesus agonized over his death; he knew it would be difficult. All of the men noted above agonized about their situations and asked God for help or for a way out. There is no shame in this. There is no reason to hide our feelings when dealing with God. If we are honest with him, he will give us the strength to face what's ahead.

....

While they headed back to the others, the missing disciple, Judas, was arriving from Jerusalem. He wasn't alone, though; with him were soldiers and guards sent by the high priest to arrest Jesus. They came with torches, clubs, and swords, as if they were out to arrest a common criminal. Judas approached Jesus and kissed him, a common

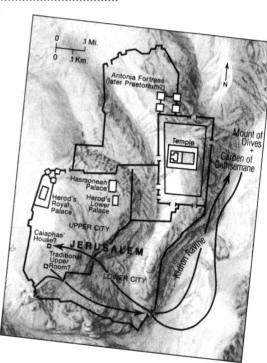

sign of greeting in the Holy Land even today. He did so to signal the guards whom they were out to get.

We shouldn't get the idea that Jesus was helpless here. He knew they were coming for him and that Judas was the one to betray him. John, wanting to make sure everyone knew Jesus was still in control, recorded that Jesus stepped up to the guards after Judas greeted him and asked whom they were looking for. When they answered "Jesus of Nazareth,"

Jesus said, "I am he." When he said this, the guards were knocked off their feet and fell backwards. After they all got up, Jesus asked his question again, and the guards answered the same as before, though maybe a little less confidently. Nothing happened this time—they remained standing.

Peter couldn't stand by and let this happen, so he grabbed his sword and struck at the person closest to him, the high priest's servant, Malchus, and cut off his ear. Jesus stopped him before anyone else got hurt. "Put your sword away. Shall I not drink the cup the Father has given me?" Then, touching Malchus's head, Jesus healed him. Jesus then submitted to the soldiers, who let the disciples go at Jesus' request.

....

These soldiers had seen a lot more than they had bargained for. Instead of just arresting a criminal or a nut, they stood face-to-face with God. Whether any of them figured out for themselves that he really was God's Son or if they all just ignored the events of that evening is unknown. It is hard to believe that this encounter would have had no effect on them. When we meet God, he touches us in a way no one else can. When we see things that can only be because of God, we can't ignore him, no matter how hard we might try. Instead of rationalizing or making up excuses for why these unusual things happen, let's admit God's behind them and give him glory.

....

42 · Jesus' Trials

MATTHEW 26:57–27:31; MARK 14:53–20;
LUKE 22:54–23:25; JOHN 18:12–19:16

Have you ever heard of circuit courts?
The term comes from the Old West,
where judges were responsible for
a large territory and would ride
a circuit to hear cases and settle legal problems. Well, Jesus
was part of a circuit court of sorts, but he—the person on
trial—was the one going from place to place, not the judge.

Between late Thursday night and Friday morning Jesus
went through six different trials before five different people
or groups. And, believe it or not, even though he had all of
these hearings, he did not receive justice.

After his arrest, the guards brought Jesus from the Garden
of Gethsemane to Annas's house in Jerusalem. Annas was the
ex–high priest, whom Rome had taken out of power and
replaced with his son-in-law, Caiaphas. Possibly as a sign of
respect to Annas (or because he still held a lot of power),
Jesus was brought to him first. This trial reached no conclu-
sions, so Jesus was sent on to Caiaphas.

Once in front of Caiaphas and the other chief priests
who gathered at his home, Jesus was interrogated. False
witness after false witness could not come up with a believ-
able story. It was at this meeting that Jesus proclaimed,
when asked if he was the Son of God, "I am, and you will
see me sitting at the right hand of God, and returning to
earth in the clouds of heaven."

Caiaphas was playing this for all it was worth. He tore his

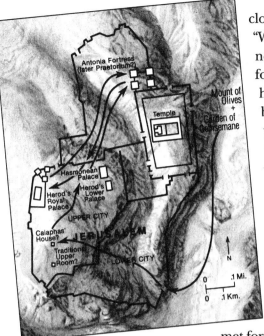

clothes and said, "What more do we need? Why wait for witnesses? You have heard his blasphemy. What is your verdict?" The vote was unanimous for the death penalty. They then blindfolded Jesus and beat him.

Later that morning, after daybreak, the Sanhedrin (the Jewish Council) met formally to sentence Jesus to death. Though Jesus had undergone three trials, none of them were legal. He was tried in the middle of the night, which was against Jewish law. He had false witnesses testify against him. And his guilt was determined by his own testimony, another violation of his civil rights. The Sanhedrin, the Jewish Supreme Court, found Jesus guilty of blasphemy, and demanded the death penalty. Since Rome had taken away their privilege of capital punishment, the leaders sent him to the Antonia Fortress to Pontius Pilate, the Roman governor, for his consent to have Jesus crucified. During Jesus' fourth trial, Pilate could find nothing against Jesus and tried to let him go. Since the Jewish leaders wouldn't let him, Pilate sent Jesus to King Herod, ruler of Galilee (the region Jesus was from). Herod was at his Jerusalem palace for the Passover.

Herod didn't really care if Jesus was innocent or guilty— he just wanted to see some miracles. When Jesus wouldn't perform for him, Herod sent him back to Pilate. Pilate questioned Jesus again at this sixth and final trial. Pilate again tried to release Jesus, but the leaders told him that if he didn't crucify Jesus, he was no friend to Caesar. Then when Pilate asked if they really wanted him to crucify their king, the chief priests yelled, "We have no king but Caesar!" Realizing this was one battle he was not going to win, Pilate finally gave in to the crowd. He gave the order for Jesus to be beaten and then crucified.

....

Though Pilate seems to get the blame for crucifying Jesus, the religious leaders carried the greater guilt. They were so wrapped up in keeping their power that they railroaded an innocent man, a man who they knew—deep down—was the Son of God. If that wasn't bad enough, they then acknowledged Caesar as their only king. They forgot that God was their king and, in professing their loyalty to Caesar, committed yet another blasphemy. Our ambitions can get in the way of not only treating others fairly but also acknowledging God. There is no greater evil we can fall into than denying God. Let's try to be honest with ourselves and keep our ambitions in check. One small lapse in class or on the sports field could be the first step toward a huge, eternal mistake.

....

43 · The Way of the Cross

MATTHEW 27:32-34; MARK 15:21-24;
LUKE 23:26-31; JOHN 19:17

O n the East Coast many inns make the boast: "George Washington slept here." Maybe he did; maybe he didn't. Some of the inns aren't even old enough for it to be true! In fact, so many places have made the claim that "George Washington slept here" that it has become a joke (and even a hysterical old Jack Benny movie).

Many of the same type of claims have been made in the Holy Land. Tour guides claim to know the exact location of Bible events and point out traditional sites even after archaeology has proven them to be incorrect. Of course, many of the tourist attractions are indeed the places they claim to be, and many more are as likely to be the biblical places as any. The places where Jesus taught and performed miracles are especially popular and sacred. They are so sacred that many of these places have churches built over them to mark the event. Some locations with churches are Jesus' birthplace in Bethlehem, Jesus' childhood home in Nazareth, and Peter's house in Capernaum where Jesus healed Peter's mother-in-law. These are just a few of many places Christians who visit these areas think of as holy. Jerusalem is no exception to this rule. Many places are believed to be actual locations of the events in Christ's life. The Upper Room, where the Last Supper was celebrated, is one such place. The pool of Bethesda, where Jesus healed a lame man, is another.

No doubt the most moving and horrifying sites are those connected with Jesus' death. After Pilate sentenced Jesus to death, Jesus was forced to carry his own cross from the Antonia Fortress (also known as the Praetorium) to the place of execution, Golgotha. The traditional route of Jesus' last moments winds eastward through the streets of Jerusalem for about a quarter of a mile; at that time, it then led outside the city wall another tenth of a mile to the hill of execution. Today Golgotha lies inside the city walls. If you visit Jerusalem, you cannot miss this historic path; the route is marked by the Stations of the Cross, fourteen positions along the way where separate incidents are commemorated. The beginning of the route, the place where Jesus stumbled, the spot where Simon of Cyrene carried the cross for Jesus, the spot where Jesus turned to the crowd and warned the women of the evils to befall humanity in the future, and others are all identified with plaques. You can even go on a tour and carry a cross along a part of the route to help you imagine a portion of what Jesus suffered.

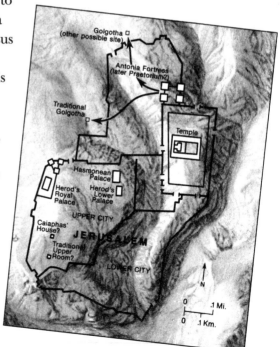

At the end of this gruesome journey was Golgotha (the Place of the Skull), where criminals were crucified. The Latin name for Golgotha is Calvary, which may be more familiar to us from hymns and church names. It was here that the soldiers nailed Jesus to the cross and gambled for his clothes. The crowds also jeered Jesus, telling him to save himself if he could save others. From the cross Jesus asked the apostle John to care for his mother. At three in the afternoon, Jesus called to God, "Father, I commit my spirit to you," and died.

Nicodemus and Joseph of Arimathea then approached Pilate and asked to bury Jesus' body. Wrapping him in a long linen cloth, they carried his body to Joseph's new tomb near the place of execution. It was here that Jesus' body lay, if for only a few days. The Church of the Holy Sepulchre marks the location of the tomb.

....

No greater act has ever been done for humanity. Jesus gave up everything earthly and submitted himself to humiliation and torture so we could escape the penalty for sin and spend eternity with God. While we celebrate Christmas and Easter, we often overlook Good Friday. The Resurrection is important, but without understanding the suffering before Jesus rose from the grave, we can sometimes take God's salvation lightly. Jesus paid a huge price to bring us salvation, and to take that gift for granted is a shame. Let's not ever take lightly what Jesus did; let's live every moment to show Christ how thankful we are.

....

44 · On the Road to Emmaus

MARK 16:12-13; LUKE 24:13-43

*S*unday: the Passover was over, Jesus was dead, and now these two followers decided to leave Jerusalem—there was nothing left for them there. With the Jesus movement behind them, they were free to go back home to Emmaus. Exactly where Emmaus was we are not sure. It was about seven miles from Jerusalem, probably west or northwest of the Jewish capital, possibly the village known as el-Qubeibah.

As these two people were walking home, Jesus joined them on their journey, though they did not recognize him. Jesus could see that they were pretty bummed out and asked them what they were talking about. "You must be the only person in Jerusalem who hasn't heard about the terrible things that happened there last week," they answered.

Playing dumb, Jesus asked, "What things?"

"The things that happened to Jesus, the Man from Nazareth. He was a Prophet who did incredible miracles and was a mighty Teacher, highly regarded by both God and man. But the chief priests and our religious leaders . . . crucified him. We had thought he was the glorious Messiah and that he had come to rescue Israel." Then they recounted for Jesus how some women in their group were saying that Jesus was alive and that the body was gone from the tomb.

Jesus answered them, "You are such foolish, foolish people! You find it so hard to believe all that the prophets wrote in the Scriptures! Wasn't it clearly predicted by the prophets that the Messiah would have to suffer all these things before entering his time of glory?" Jesus spent the rest of the trip citing them example after example of prophecy that described all that had happened to him.

Evening came, and they reached Emmaus. Jesus was planning on moving on, but the disciples insisted that he come and have dinner with them. Agreeing, Jesus went to their home. After he gave thanks for the food, he broke the bread. Then, they recognized this man to be Jesus, and, as they did, he disappeared. They were so excited that they immediately rushed back to Jerusalem, despite it being dark and the roads dangerous.

....

How excited are we to tell others about Jesus being raised from the dead? Is it something we can't wait to do? Would we even skip dinner and walk several miles to tell our friends about it? Or is it more of the kind of news we mention only when we have to? The news of Jesus' victory over death is the biggest, best news we can ever tell anyone—even bigger than if the Cubs were to ever win the World Series! Hopefully, we are

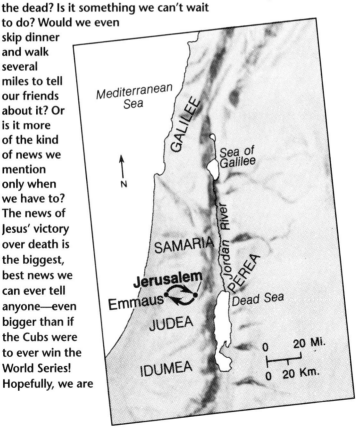

still excited enough about it to tell our family and friends. News like this is way too good to keep to ourselves.

....

When these disciples returned to the Upper Room in Jerusalem, they were greeted with the news that Jesus had also appeared to Peter! They then told their story, amazing everyone. Then, Jesus appeared in the room with them. *We must be seeing a ghost,* they all thought.

"Why are you frightened?" Jesus asked them. He then showed them his feet and hands to prove that it was really he.

Still they weren't sure. Oh that it could be true, but how?

Then, to prove conclusively that he wasn't a ghost, Jesus asked for something to eat. When he ate some fish, their doubt vanished. Ghosts could never eat! Jesus really was alive!

45 · Philip Paves the Way

ACTS 6:1-5; 8:1-41; 21:8-9

Philip's story is a story of firsts. He might not be the most-remembered person in the Bible, but he contributed a lot to the early church.

The first of the firsts was that Philip was one of the first seven men called to be deacons in Jerusalem. The men chosen had to be "wise and full of the Holy Spirit, who are well thought of by everyone." The other six men were Stephen (who was martyred soon afterward), Prochorus, Nicanor, Timon, Parmenas, and Nicolaus of Antioch.

....

These seven deacons needed to be wise and full of the Spirit, but their main job wasn't that spiritual: They were to feed Greek widows in Jerusalem. They weren't supposed to preach or witness (although they did this all the time without being told to); they were there to make sure people ate. No one is above any job in the church. These men were the wisest and most spiritual—and they were to feed widows. A former football star tells that when he couldn't make church because of the games, his job in the church was to clean the washrooms on Saturday. Let's not think that just because we're straight-A students or sports stars or homecoming queens that we are too good to do any job. All work can bring glory to God.

....

Philip was also the first guy (since Jesus) to preach to the Samaritans. The Jews hated the Samaritans and must have thought Philip crazy for preaching to these horrible people. While in the city of Samaria (the former capital of the evil northern kingdom of Israel), Philip led many people to Christ and baptized them. The apostles in Jerusalem heard

about this and sent
Peter and John to
check it out. Seeing
that Samaritans
really were accept-
ing Christ, they
laid hands on the
believers, who then
received the Holy
Spirit just as the
Jews had. Peter
and John were
so happy that
they stopped at
several Samaritan
villages on the
way back to Jeru-
salem to preach
instead of hurry-
ing through the
region so they

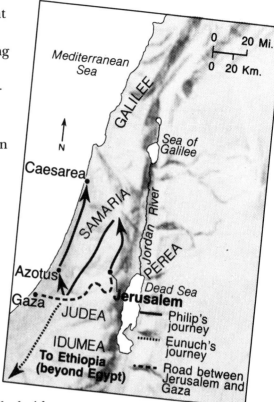

wouldn't have to deal with
these "unclean" people any more than necessary.

Philip is probably best known for his visit with an Ethiopian eunuch who was on his way back home from Jerusalem.
This was quite an event, both for Philip and for the Ethiopian. While Philip was still in Samaria, God told him to go
down to the road that led from Jerusalem to Gaza, a city
southeast of Jerusalem along the Mediterranean. Philip
reached that road around noon, just as God said, and saw an
Ethiopian in a chariot driving by.

Philip walked alongside the chariot and heard the Ethiopian reading from the prophet Isaiah.

"Do you understand it?" Philip asked.

"Of course not! How can I when there is no one to instruct

me?" the Ethiopian answered. He then asked Philip to come into the chariot and explain what he was trying to read.

Starting where the Ethiopian was reading, which was Isaiah 53:7-8, about Jesus being led as a sheep to the slaughter, he explained this and many other Scriptures to tell him about Christ.

"Look! Water!" the Ethiopian exclaimed. "Why can't I be baptized?"

When he told Philip he believed that Jesus is the Son of God, Philip agreed to baptize him. He was so happy that he rejoiced all the way to Ethiopia, which was south of Egypt, by the mouth of the Red Sea. (It's probable that this Ethiopian started a church in Ethiopia and helped the spread of the Good News.)

....

The true impact of telling one person about Christ can never really be understood. Philip told this one man who most likely went home, started a church, and helped convert a nation. Maybe the next person we tell about Christ could go on to become the next Billy Graham. But what if we don't talk to that person about Jesus? The world could miss out on a wonderful ministry. It's just like an old shampoo commercial: If we tell two friends, they'll tell two friends, and so on, and so on, and so on. . . .

....

After the Ethiopian left, Philip was suddenly and mysteriously taken to Azotus, a city that used to be the Philistine city of Ashdod. From there, Philip took more conventional methods of transportation—his feet—to travel up the coast to Caesarea, stopping in many of the towns along the way to share about Christ. He settled in Caesarea, later to host the apostle Paul on his way back to Jerusalem. It is in Acts 21:8 that we see the last of Philip's firsts—he is the first person to have four daughters who were prophetesses. These are the first women we read of in the New Testament who received messages from the Lord and shared them with others. Philip must have felt proud and privileged to have been a part of so many firsts!

46 · Paul Changes Careers
ACTS 9:1-30

Does being a CIA agent sound cool? You know, traveling to distant countries to catch criminals and bring them to justice? If so, you'd have loved Paul's job. Paul really was only a Pharisee, but he went above and beyond the call of pharisaical duty to hunt down Christians. He went to the high priest in Jerusalem and asked for extradition papers so he could go to Damascus and bring back any Christians in chains. The high priest thought this a noble, worthy task, and he agreed.

The trip to Damascus, in the Roman province of Syria, was about 180 miles, so Paul had some time on his hands to think about what he was going to do in Damascus and about all that he'd already done to stamp out the Christian church. He gave approval to the stoning of Stephen and was probably a prominent figure in the persecution of believers in Jerusalem (see Acts 6:8–8:1).

As he and his band of deputies neared Damascus around noon, a bright light from heaven shone down on Paul. The noontime sun in the desert is a huge, bright ball, but this light overpowered the sun. It was so bright it blinded him, and he fell to the ground in confusion.

A disembodied voice called to him, "Paul! Paul! Why are you persecuting me?"

"Who is speaking, sir?" Paul asked.

"I am Jesus, the one you are persecuting! Now get up and go into the city and await my further instructions."

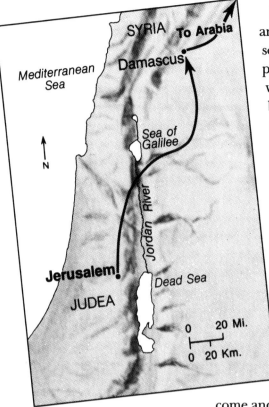

Paul was blind and confused, and so were his companions. They weren't physically blind, but spiritually, for they heard a voice coming from the light, but they couldn't understand it. They led him into Damascus, where he fasted and prayed for three days, waiting for a man called Ananias to come and heal him.

Very reluctantly, Ananias went to the house where Paul was staying on Straight Street. This street is still in Damascus, and you can see the site where Paul is believed to have stayed. Ananias arrived, laid his hands on Paul, and then baptized him. Paul, the foremost persecutor, was now a Christian.

....

Our first encounters with God are rarely this dramatic. Usually we hear about Jesus in church, or from a friend or family member. When faced with a light brighter than the sun and the actual voice of Jesus, Paul's evidence for the deity of Jesus was unquestionable. But for us or for those we tell about Jesus, the argument is never this clear-cut. We have to rely on witnesses for information about Jesus, and the best witnesses are those in the Bible. To truly be convinced of Jesus' reality, read the Bible

to see the eyewitness accounts. Reading the Bible can help you lead someone to Christ, too, because you'll be able to tell them of the wonderful ways he spoke to others.

....

Paul was an ambitious, zealous Pharisee, and now that he was a Christian, he did not lose those personality traits. He was ambitious and zealous right from the start. He went immediately to the synagogue in Damascus and told the Jews there about what happened. He astounded those who heard him. "Hey! This guy came here to arrest Jesus' followers, and now he's become one of them." No doubt the Jews thought him crazy.

Paul spent about three years in Damascus and in Arabia, a desert region southeast of Damascus, studying and telling others about Jesus. Finally the Jews in Damascus couldn't stand Paul anymore. He was too good at convincing others that Jesus was God's Son. So, in the fine tradition of Jewish leaders of the day, they tried to kill him. Paul heard of their plan, and at night some of the believers helped him escape by lowering him outside the city walls in a basket.

It would still be many years before Paul would become the trusted and beloved missionary we know him to have been. He went back to Jerusalem, only to be mistrusted by the believers there. Gradually they accepted him, but he had to leave because the Jews there were trying to kill him. The Jerusalem church arranged to send Paul to his hometown of Tarsus on the northeastern shore of the Mediterranean in Asia Minor. There Paul would stay for about eight years, studying and perfecting his evangelism skills.

....

Even Paul didn't become a great evangelist right away. While he did not wait to start telling others about Jesus, he didn't really begin to see many results until many years after his conversion. When we are having trouble telling others about Jesus, or we aren't seeing many results from the witnessing we do, we can remember Paul. If it took one of the "greatest" missionaries years to become great, we can cut ourselves some slack, too.

....

47 · Peter Tours the Holy Land

Acts 8:1-25; 9:32–10:48

A postles were highly mobile guys. Notice they were not upwardly mobile, like yuppies; they were just mobile, traveling from one area to another to spread the gospel. And while most of the original apostles were traveling all over the eastern world, we really only read about what Peter did early in his ministry.

As you may remember from Philip the Evangelist's story, he was preaching to the Samaritans, and Peter and John came to see if Samaritans really were becoming Christians. They were pleasantly surprised to see that it was true, but none of them had received the Holy Spirit yet. So the apostles prayed for them and laid their hands on the Samaritans, who then received the Spirit.

A man who had been following Philip, Simon the magician, saw the power Peter and John had to give the Spirit and begged them, "Let me have this power, too, so that when I lay my hands on people, they will receive the Holy Spirit!"

Peter's reaction was not the one he was looking for. "Your money perish with you for thinking God's gift can be bought! You can have no part in this, for your heart is not right before God. Turn from this great wickedness and pray. Perhaps God will yet forgive your evil thoughts—for I can see that there is jealousy and sin in your heart."

....

This can be a scary passage. We read that Simon was a Christian and was baptized, but then Peter tells him he's going to perish because of the sin in his heart. This raises some questions: Was

Simon really a Christian? Can Christians lose their salvation? Theologians have been debating that last question for centuries, and it cannot be answered here. But it is obvious that Simon did have sin that he hadn't confessed or conquered. That sin, if allowed to continue, would seriously harm Simon's spiritual life, perhaps even leading him to deny Christ. If we remain sensitive to confessing our sins and keep working at staying close to God, we will have little to worry about.

....

After Peter and John returned from preaching in Samaritan villages on the way back to Jerusalem, Peter toured Judea, visiting the converts. As he made his way from city to city, he performed some incredible miracles. In Lydda, Peter healed Aeneas, a man who had been paralyzed for eight years. This was so amazing to the people there that everyone in Lydda and nearby Sharon became Christians. Next, Peter went to the seaport village of Joppa (modern-day Jaffa). Here he raised Dorcas, a godly and charitable woman, from the dead as her friends prepared her for burial. Again, many here believed in Jesus because of Peter's miracle.

Peter stayed in Joppa for a while, living with a tanner. While there,

Peter had a vision of a sheet full of unclean animals, which was like a forbidden buffet. A voice told Peter to eat any he wanted to, but he refused. The voice told him, "If I say something is clean, it's clean!" This happened three times, then the sheet went back to heaven. While Peter was trying to figure this dream out, God spoke to him again. "Three men have come to see you. Go down and meet them and go with them. All is well, I have sent them."

Sure enough, three men immediately came to the door looking for Peter. They explained that they worked for Cornelius, a godly Roman centurion who was told by an angel to send for Peter. Peter believed them and set out for Cornelius's home in Caesarea the next day.

When Peter reached Cornelius's house, he told everyone there, "You know it is against the Jewish laws for me to come into a Gentile home like this. But God has shown me in a vision that I should never think of anyone as inferior. So I came as soon as I was sent for." After listening to Cornelius, Peter made a startling (for him!) observation: "I see very clearly that the Jews are not God's only favorites! In every nation he has those who worship him and do good deeds and are acceptable to him." Then, after Peter told everyone there about Jesus, the entire household believed and was baptized. Thus, we see the first Gentile converts to Christianity.

....

Peter's observation is true for us today as well. Of course we know that other nations, not just Jews, can become Christians. But the Jewish prejudice against Gentiles is really no different from our prejudices against those who are not Christians. The school bully, the cheerleader who has a reputation, the kid who sits next to you in social studies and smells of pot—they are all eligible to enter heaven. They just need someone to tell them about it. Are we willing to overcome our prejudices and talk to these "unsavable" people? Peter would want us to.

....

48 · Paul's First Missionary Journey
ACTS 13:1–14:28

Paul, Barnabas, and others were teaching and preaching in the Syrian city of Antioch. While they were there, the Holy Spirit spoke to the church leaders there, "Dedicate Barnabas and Paul for a special job I have for them." After praying, fasting, and laying their hands on the two men, the leaders sent Barnabas and Paul on their first missionary journey, which is creatively called "Paul's first missionary journey."

Their first stop on this thirteen-hundred-mile journey was at the island of Cyprus. They preached their way from east to west across the island, with the first noteworthy event occurring in Paphos. There the Roman governor, Sergius Paulus, wanted to hear what Paul and Barnabas had to say. But a magician named Elymas opposed them and tried to persuade Paulus to ignore the Christians' teachings. This ticked Paul off, to put it mildly. Filled with the Spirit, he yelled at Elymas, "You son of the devil, . . . will you never end your opposition to the Lord? And now God has laid his hand of punishment upon you, and you will be stricken awhile with blindness." This was quite a demonstration of God's power; as a result, Sergius Paulus believed.

After this, the missionaries sailed to Perga on the coast of central Asia Minor. It was here that John Mark left Paul and his uncle Barnabas and returned home. (He was either homesick, angered that Gentiles were being converted, or mad

because Paul was taking over the leadership of the team from
Uncle Barnabas). Paul and Barnabas headed north to Antioch in the region of Pisidia, not the Antioch they started
from. The two men preached in the synagogue there, converting many, including a lot of Gentiles, who were very
happy to be part of God's plan. But, as was the case so often
with Jesus and the apostles, the Jewish leaders became jealous
of their popularity and chased them out of town.

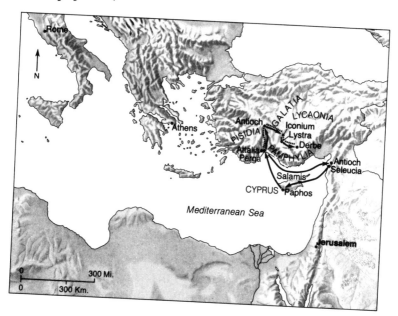

So the missionaries headed southeast to the town of
Iconium. They stayed there for a while and convinced many
of the truth of Jesus' resurrection. Some did not believe the
story though, and they organized a mob to stone the two.
Running for their lives, Paul and Barnabas kept heading
southeast to the town of Lystra.

In Lystra, Paul and Barnabas were greeted with great
enthusiasm when they healed a crippled man because they
were believed to be gods. The crowds thought Barnabas was
Jupiter, the supreme Roman god, and Paul was Mercury, the

messenger, better known today as the FTD flower guy. It was all Paul and Barnabas could do to stop the crowds from sacrificing to them. Then, as often happens with popular acclaim, the crowds turned on them. Some Jews who had followed Paul from Antioch incited a mob against Paul, stoned him, and dragged him outside the city, leaving him for dead. Paul then, to everyone's surprise, stood up, dusted himself off, and headed back into the city.

....

Nothing worth doing is ever easy. It's a cliché, but it's true. And if that thing you're doing is for God, you can believe that the job will be twice as hard. It could have been very tempting for Paul to just say, "Forget it!" after he came very close to dying for being a missionary. But he hung in there and helped many people become Christians. Commitment is important to any task. Before we even start, we should ask ourselves, Can we stay in it when the going gets tough? Will we be tough and get going, as the saying goes, or will we lie down and give up? If we are truly committed to our task, God will give us strength to continue and will help us over the rough spots.

....

From Lystra they went on to Derbe and won many converts to Christ. Then they headed back the way they came, strengthening the new Christians in the cities they had visited before and appointing leaders in each new church. They worked their way back to Perga, then preached in Attalia, where they had not stopped when they first arrived in Asia Minor, and then caught a ship back to Antioch.

49 · Paul's Second Missionary Journey

ACTS 15:1–18:22

A great council had just recessed in Jerusalem. One group, the Judaizers, said Gentiles had to follow Jewish laws, while another group, led by Paul, said that Christ released everyone from the ceremonial laws the Jews tried so hard to obey. The council decided to place minimal requirements on the new believers, and Paul and Barnabas accompanied the letter with the verdict to Antioch. Everyone in Antioch was happy to get the news.

Later, Paul and Barnabas decided to visit the churches they had helped start in Asia Minor to see how they were faring. But when Barnabas wanted to bring John Mark, who had deserted them on the first trip, Paul wouldn't stand for it and the two split up. Barnabas and Mark traveled to Cyprus, and Paul joined with Silas, one of the messengers from the Jerusalem council.

Paul and Silas headed north, then west to Derbe and Lystra, two of the last towns Paul visited on the first journey. It was in Lystra that Paul met Timothy, a young man whom Paul invited to join them. They then went on to Troas. It was here that Luke most likely joined Paul; we assume this because it is here that Luke, the author of Acts, starts using *we* instead of *they* as he tells his story. It was also here that Paul received a vision of a Macedonian man who called to them, "Come over here and help us." That settled it; they would go to new territory—Greece.

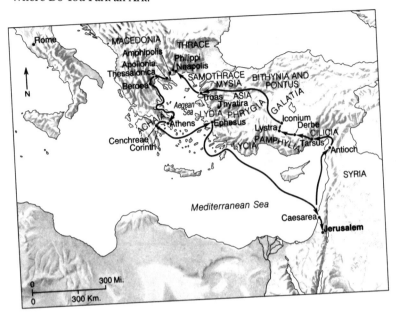

After they reached shore, they went to Philippi, an important city on the eastern border of Macedonia. A woman named Lydia was there on business from Thyatira. She heard God's message and believed, she and her whole household. It was also in Philippi that Paul cast a demon out of a slave girl. Her masters saw what happened and, instead of being happy for her, were angry that they could no longer make money from her satanic arts. They grabbed Paul and Silas and brought them before the judges, who had them whipped and beaten, then thrown in jail.

As Paul and Silas were chained in that prison, they sang hymns and prayed to God. Suddenly a great earthquake shook the prison, causing the doors to open and the chains to fall off the prisoners. The guard thought everyone had escaped and was preparing to take his life because if you lost a prisoner, you would have to pay his sentence. But Paul stopped him: "Don't do it! We are all here!"

Then, after hearing the men sing and pray, and after

seeing everyone stay put even when they could have escaped, the jailer asked Paul, "What must I do to be saved?"

"Believe in the Lord Jesus and you will be saved, and your entire household," was their answer. The jailer then brought Paul and Silas to his home, washed their wounds, and was baptized along with his whole family.

....

That's all there is to becoming a Christian—believing in Jesus! No difficult rules to follow, no secret phrases of initiation, no papers to sign. Just belief that he is God's Son who came to take away our sin. If you believe that, congratulations! You're a Christian! It is necessary to learn more about God and possibly change some habits, but that comes later. All we need to do to become a Christian is believe. If we're trying to share Jesus with others, let's remember that they need to see God's love so they can love him too. They don't need to hear rules and regulations.

....

Once they were released from prison, they went to Thessalonica, where a mob of jealous Jews started a riot, attacking the man who let Paul and Silas stay with him. Paul escaped and went to Beroea, where the people were open to the gospel. But some Jews followed Paul from Thessalonica and created trouble in Beroea, so he moved on to Athens, in southeastern Greece. Here he debated with the philosophers on Mars Hill; they thought him crazed, but a few believed him. Moving on, Paul and his group stayed in Corinth for a year and a half, after God encouraged him in a vision, "Don't be afraid! Speak out! Don't quit! For I am with you and no one can harm you." Shortly after another riot in a synagogue, Paul left for Ephesus, where he preached for a short time before heading on to Jerusalem for a feast. After the feast, Paul returned to Antioch, ending his second missionary journey.

50 · Paul's Third Missionary Journey

ACTS 18:23–21:17

By now I'm sure we're all becoming familiar with the places Paul visited on his first two missionary trips. On the third and final recorded journey, he visited most of them again, encouraging and teaching the believers there. Here, then, are the highlights from Paul's last, and longest, missionary journey.

Ephesus: Paul meets disciples of John the Baptist and tells them about events since John. They accept Christ, are baptized, and receive the Holy Spirit. Also, the seven sons of Sceva try to exorcise a demon, saying to it, "I adjure you by Jesus, whom Paul preaches, to come out!" The demon answers, "I know Jesus and I know Paul, but who are you?" and then tears the brothers' clothes and beats them up. Aside from the humorous nature of this account, this prompts many in this city to burn their books of black magic and idols. When those who make the idols learn of this and of Paul's activities, they abduct Paul's companions and try to hold a trial. The mayor, however, manages to calm everyone down by asserting the power of the goddess Diana to fend for herself and by warning them about the Roman troops who are eager to put down riots and revolts. He then has everyone go home.

Greece: Paul learns of yet another plot against his life, so he heads back north to Macedonia instead of sailing for Syria from near Athens.

Troas: After staying there for a week, Paul preaches an

150

evening sermon the night before they are to leave. They all meet in a crowded upper room lit by lamps. At midnight, the heat in the room and the late hour get the better of a young man named Eutychus, who falls asleep and topples from the window ledge he was sitting on, falling three stories to his death. Paul does not seem concerned—he goes down, heals the man, and then brings everyone back inside so he can finish his message!

....

There are two schools of thought about this incident. Lay people view this as a sign from God that it's OK to fall asleep during church. Pastors, on the other hand, feel that this proves even death shouldn't keep you from hearing the end of their sermon.

....

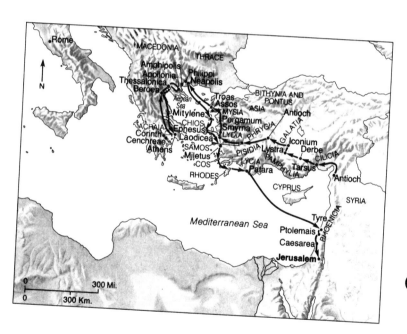

Miletus: The Ephesian elders meet with Paul here since he will not have time to go to Ephesus. He gives them words of instruction, since he isn't sure what lies ahead in Jerusalem or if he'll make it back to Ephesus. It's a touching scene: They pray together and cry over their parting.

Caesarea: Near the end of the trip. They stay at Philip's house for several days. While there, Agabus, a prophet, approaches Paul, takes Paul's belt, ties his own feet and hands, and proclaims, "The Holy Spirit declares, 'So shall the owner of this belt be bound by the Jews in Jerusalem and turned over to the Romans.'" Everyone is upset, except for Paul. He tries reasoning with his friends, "Why all this weeping? . . . For I am ready not only to be jailed at Jerusalem but also to die for the sake of the Lord Jesus."

Jerusalem: Not long after the prediction of Paul's problems here, they arrive in Jerusalem. Their reception is friendly. But what do the next days hold?

....

If someone told us we'd be arrested and persecuted when we get to where we're going, would we change plans? I'd be really tempted to. Paul never even entertained the notion. Whatever God had in store for him was OK by him. He willingly suffered whatever his enemies threw his way. The only way to remain strong in such times is by complete, total, unwavering faith. Hopefully, someday if we find ourselves in a similar situation, we will be able to show the same dependence and faith in God that Paul showed.

....

51 · **Paul Sails to Rome**

ACTS 21:18–28:31

Imagine being accused of doing something really bad by a classmate. The teacher makes you stand in the hall for a while and then comes out to hear what you have to say for yourself. But before the teacher can say if you're in trouble or not, you proclaim, "I want to go to the principal! Let's let him decide." Pretty nuts, huh? Nuts or not, this is in effect what the apostle Paul did.

Paul got in trouble with the Jewish leaders. They said he brought a Gentile into the inner court of the Temple, which was punishable by death. Paul's enemies yelled their accusations to the people in the streets, who, appalled at such sacrilege, tried to kill Paul. A Roman commander rescued Paul and took him into custody. After a riotous meeting of the Jewish Council, forty Jews vowed not to eat or drink again until they had killed Paul. Learning of the plot, the commander ordered two hundred soldiers, plus spearmen and cavalry, to take Paul to Governor Felix in Caesarea. Felix heard the case against Paul, didn't find him guilty, but held him in prison for two years, hoping to receive a bribe from Paul. By the end of his term as governor, Paul still hadn't bought him off, so Felix left him in prison for the new governor to handle. Festus asked Paul if he'd stand trial in Jerusalem (where people were still eager to kill him). Paul answered, "No! I demand my privilege of a hearing before the emperor himself. . . . *I appeal to Caesar.*"

153

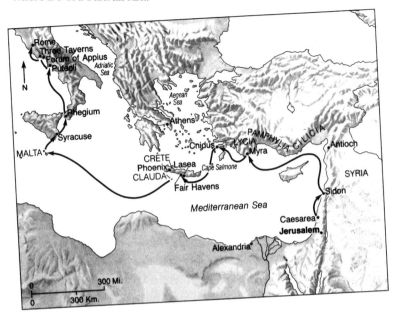

Paul had appealed, and there was nothing to do after that except to take him to Rome for his hearing. A huge grain ship carried Paul, his friends Aristarchus and Luke, other prisoners, guards, and crew to many ports in Asia Minor, today called Turkey. Because of these constant stops to buy and sell goods, the trip took longer than if going straight to Rome. Even if the ship never made any stops, it would have followed the same basic course because captains never wanted to sail too far away from land in case an emergency arose, such as a storm or a leak. (Airplanes crossing the Atlantic follow the same principle—they fly along the East Coast to Greenland, then across to England or Germany.)

As it just so happened, an emergency did arise. It was late in the sailing season, probably early to mid-November. As they left Sidon in Syria and headed west, they encountered stronger and stronger winds. They continued on, heading toward the island of Crete, and stopping in the port at Fair Havens. The ship docked for a few days, but then headed out on a pleasant day, despite Paul's warnings and the fact that the season was about over. The weather changed, with a strong wind pushing the ship out to sea, not allowing them to sail along the Greek coast. The storm grew in strength. The crew threw over the cargo to lighten the load. After two weeks, no one had eaten anything, and everyone was weakened. Paul urged them all to eat, for they needed their strength. The next day they sighted land, though no one recognized the coast. But as the saying goes, "Any port in a storm." They tried to steer the ship between the rocks in the bay. They couldn't. The ship hit a sandbar and stuck, with the waves gradually breaking the ship apart. Julius, Paul's guard, wouldn't let the guards kill the prisoners (to make sure no one escaped) and instead ordered everyone to swim to shore under his own strength.

The island everyone swam to safely was Malta; no one recognized the coast because it was well off the normal Rome-Egypt trading route. As Paul was gathering sticks for a fire, a snake slithered out and bit him on the hand. Even though the snake was poisonous, Paul just shook it off. This wasn't the only miracle that happened here, though. The governor's father was very sick, and Paul healed him. Word spread over the island, and people came from all over to be healed. After three months, when the sailing season began again in mid to late February, they boarded a ship that wintered there and sailed north, passing between Sicily and Italy's big toe, eventually reaching Rome.

....

At the writing of Acts, Paul had been in Rome two years and was still a prisoner awaiting trial. When God said Paul would go to Rome, I'm sure Paul never thought that he would be in chains or that it would take him over two years to get there. On the bright side, though, Paul didn't have to pay the fare for the ride to Rome. God's timing seems rather peculiar sometimes and inconvenient at others. Whether or not we can make sense out of it, God can and does. He controls time and events. We can only take the opportunities God allows us, hoping and praying they are for the best. And if they are God's, they are for the best!

....

155

52 · The Seven Churches of Revelation

REVELATION 2–3

The apostle John was an old man facing what amounted to life imprisonment on Patmos, a small, rocky island in the Aegean Sea.

His crime was that of speaking about Jesus; his punishment was by the Roman Empire. While Rome did manage to keep John in one location, they could not silence him nor keep him away from his God. It was during his exile on this island that John had a vision, a vision of such importance and complexity that people today are still trying to figure out what it all means!

This vision was of the end of the world, of spiritual battles and strange beasts: It was *The Revelation*. The church in John's time was facing many problems: The Romans were persecuting Christians, local merchants were fighting them because they didn't want to lose their idol-making businesses, and false teachers were misleading many. John, in fact, was fortunate to only be in exile; many were killed for their faith (all of the other apostles are traditionally believed to have been killed for their belief in Christ). It was for this vision that John was kept alive. And this vision was Jesus' message to his church that no matter how bad things got, no matter how many spiritual battles they fought, God would win the war.

The book of Revelation was actually a letter sent to seven churches in western Asia Minor. The order in which the churches were addressed reflected the messenger's route to the churches. You see, there was a circular road that connected all of the cities Christ had a message for. So, when the messenger delivered John's letter, he would land at Ephesus, which was on the Aegean coast, about fifty miles northeast of Patmos. He would take the letter to the church leaders there. When they were finished reading it, the messenger would then head north along the coast to Smyrna. Then he would continue along the road to Pergamos, Thyatira, Sardis, Philadelphia, and finally Laodicea. From Laodicea he would then head west and return to Ephesus. All told, the trip around that circle was about 350 miles.

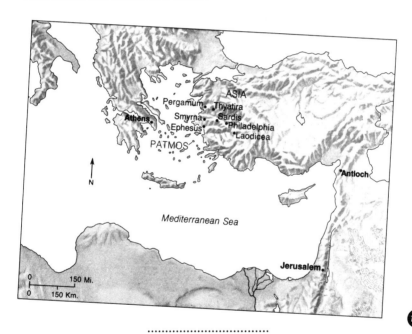

....

God is a God of order. He arranged the distribution of this letter in the most organized, efficient manner possible. If you doubt God's concern over the details of your life, just look at this simple example of how God was looking after the details of this messenger's life. This isn't as dramatic an example as rescuing someone from prison, but it is just as real. Try to look for the ways God has brought order to your life, even if it is only something as ordinary as arranging all your classes

close to your locker. Thank him for caring about the small things of your life; you can bet the messenger of Revelation did!

....

The churches may all have been glad to get a glimpse of the future (even as confusing as it is), but not all were so happy about each of their messages, for all of the letters weren't positive. Ephesus didn't come out too badly in comparison to some other churches. The Ephesians were hard workers, haters of sin, and testers of those who taught them. But they had lost the intensity of their love for God. Jesus warned them to recapture the love they first felt for him. Smyrna was having lots of earthly problems, but Christ did not fault them. He commended them for putting up with poverty and slander, and warned them to stay faithful during the coming persecution. If they could keep their faith in him, even if faced with death, they would receive the crown of life—life with Jesus and God. Those in Pergamos were loyal to Christ, but they were allowing false teachers to influence the believers there.

Thyatira's church (possibly started by Lydia, who was converted by Paul) was full of good deeds, love, and patience; but they, too, allowed a false teacher to corrupt the church. Those who followed this Jezebel were urged to repent or suffer the consequences. Sardis looked alive, but Christ said this church was dead. Doing Christian things wasn't enough; they needed to cleanse the sin from their church so they looked good deep down, not just on the surface. Philadelphia was doing well, even though the church wasn't strong. But they tried to obey, and they did not deny Jesus. Jesus promised to protect this church in the time of "Great Tribulation." The Laodiceans were in the worst shape—they were rich and complacent, lukewarm toward the things of God. They didn't hate God, they just were indifferent to him. (Today we'd call these people "nominal Christians"—Christians in name only, not deeds.)

....

Do any of these churches sound familiar to you? Are any like our churches? Or like us? If so, let's hope we look like the church of Smyrna, which was faithful even in times of trouble, or like Philadelphia, which at least tried to obey God, even if it couldn't succeed all the time. We need to ask Jesus to keep us strong and help us and our churches to model the good churches listed here.

....

Look for this additional Bible Quest volume!

HOPE IN A SCARLET ROPE
Kingsley M. Baehr 0-8423-1345-1
Intriguing stories of unsung Bible heroes will help you apply important biblical lessons to contemporary life.

Additional resources for the issues in your life:

DEATH & BEYOND
James Watkins 0-8423-1278-1
The author's research and interviews with people who deal with death daily offer a biblical perspective on questions about life and death.

IF I COULD ASK GOD *ONE* QUESTION ...
Greg Johnson 0-8423-1616-7
These truthful, biblically based answers to spiritual questions will help you build a stronger faith.

IN TOUCH
Get into God's Word with these devotional excerpts from *The Living Bible*.
   Softcover   0-8423-1710-4
   Deluxe Gift Edition   0-8423-1711-2

KEEPING YOUR COOL WHILE SHARING YOUR FAITH
Greg Johnson and Susie Shellenberger   0-8423-7036-6
Advice, humor, and encouragement to help you share your faith—from authors who speak a teen's language.

SO YOU WANT SOLUTIONS   0-8423-6161-8
SO YOU WANT TO GET INTO THE RACE   0-8423-6082-4
Chuck Klein
Designed for individual or group study, these guides will help you build and live out a strong Christian faith.

WHAT HIGH SCHOOL STUDENTS SHOULD KNOW ABOUT CREATION   0-8423-7872-3
WHAT HIGH SCHOOL STUDENTS SHOULD KNOW ABOUT EVOLUTION   0-8423-7873-1
Kenneth N. Taylor
Logic and scriptural principles support a Christian viewpoint on the creation vs. evolution issue.

Fantastic!
That's what teens are saying about the *Life Application Bible for Students*. Written and edited by the nation's leading youth experts, this one-of-a-kind Bible addresses the issues you face every day. Available in *The Living Bible* and New King James Version.